Anglican Swahili
Prayer Books:

Tanzania (1995) and Congo (1998)

by
Ian Tarrant

Senior Anglican Chaplain, University of Nottingham

Honorary Canon of the Cathedral of St Apolo Kivebulaya,
Boga, Democratic Republic of Congo

Contents

Abbreviations used when referring to sources of liturgy:

1549, 1662 – Respective *Books of Common Prayer* of the Church of England

A1979 – *Book of Common Prayer* (Episcopal Church, New York, 1979)

ASB - *Alternative Service Book* (Church of England, Oxford, 1980)

C1998 - *Kitabu cha Sala kwa Watu Wote* (Province de l'Eglise Anglican du Congo, 1998)

CW – *Common Worship Services and Prayers for the Church of England* (CHP, London, 2000)

K2002 - Anglican Church of Kenya, *Our Modern Services* (Uzima, Nairobi, 2002) NB This is the hardback collection of services, some of which were published earlier in booklet form, beginning with *A Modern Service of Holy Communion* in 1989.

NZ1989 - Church of the Province of New Zealand, *A New Zealand Prayer Book* (Collins, Auckland, 1989)

Series 3 - Church of England, *Alternative Services, Series 3* (London)

T1986 - *Kitabu cha Sala, Kanisa la Jimbo la Tanzania* (Central Tanganyika Press, Dodoma, 1986)

T1995 – *Kitabu cha Sala, Kanisa la Jimbo la Tanzania* (Central Tanganyika Press, Dodoma, 1995)

Z1994 – *Kitabu cha Sala kwa Watu Wote* (Communauté Anglicane du Zaïre, 1994)

When quoting a source for a liturgical text, I may qualify the reference with:

cp – 'minor changes made' (perhaps for aesthetic reasons)

ad – 'adapted from' (changes to theological content or emphasis)

(Note that where similar texts exist in, for example, 1662, 1928 and ASB, after translation into Swahili it is not always possible to tell which text was the starting point.)

Other abbreviations:
    BCMS - Bible Churchmen's Missionary Society (latterly Crosslinks)
    CMS - Church Missionary Society (latterly Church Mission Society)
    ISThA – Institut Supérieur Théologique Anglican
    UMCA - Universities Mission to Central Africa

THE COVER PICTURE

Shows the location of Congo and Tanzania on a map of Africa with the covers of their respective Anglican Prayer Books.

First Impression December 2006

ISSN 0951-2667
ISBN 978-1-85311-802-9

Introduction

This study attempts to compare liturgical revision in Anglican churches in two neighbouring, but quite different African countries, which together straddle Africa from west to east.

The prayer book of the Anglican Church of Kenya, *Our Modern Services* (K2002), has attracted a good deal of attention, but that is because it was compiled in English, and has circulated around the world.[1] However, with the books under consideration in this Study, on the other hand, few people outside Congo or Tanzania will have seen them, and fewer still will have been able to read them, since they are written in Swahili. They have not been publicized, known, studied or appreciated elsewhere in the Anglican Communion[2], and this Study is an attempt to redress that lack.

Why are you reading this Study? You may be reading to learn about the diversity of God's church and how it worships. True worship should reflect the joys and concerns of the worshipper, so a prayer book *ought* to give a glimpse of the heart of the church.

Alternatively you may be reading to learn from the experiences of two national churches engaging with their contexts and heritages, in the hope of finding wisdom or texts of which you can make use in your own situation.

Thirdly, you may be reading for the pure joy of discovering new things about God's creation and his church.

For my part, I was deeply involved in the revision process for Congo during my years as an expatriate priest of the diocese of Boga. Apart from other international links with Swahili-speaking countries, I also had the privilege of representing the Province of Zaire (as it then was) at the CAPA Liturgical Consultation at Kanamai in Kenya in June 1993. The Statement by the Consultation was useful for all the countries of Africa, and helps provide us with a standard against which to compare the work done in both Tanzania and Congo.[3] I should add how grateful I am to all the people who helped in various ways to make this Study possible.

[1]   The various stages of compiling this book have also been written up in this series – see Graham Kings and Geoff Morgan, *Offerings from Kenya to Anglicanism* (Alcuin/GROW Joint Liturgical Study 50, Grove Books, Cambridge, 2001).
[2]   Rare 'international' occasions have aired them, as, e.g., an earlier version of the Tanzanian Liturgy, in Swahili, was used for the opening eucharist of the 1978 Lambeth Conference; and the Congo eucharist of 1998 was used in an English translation at ACC-13 in Nottingham in 2005.
[3]   See report edited by Gitari (details in Bibliography) which includes the Statement.

1. Tanzania

1.1 History - the last 500 years

The first Europeans to arrive on the coast of what we now call Tanzania were the Portuguese, and they found a complex society already in existence. Along the coast there was a flourishing economy of small states, self-sufficient in food, thanks to fishing and agriculture, but also trading spices, craft goods, ivory and slaves with each other and with countries around the rim of the Indian Ocean. The culture drew on Arabia and Islam; Arabic and Swahili were used for communication, and both were written using Arabic script.

Zanzibar was the largest of many islands along the coast, and was ruled by the Portuguese from 1503 to 1698, then by the Sultan of Oman until 1861, when the Sultanate was divided between two brothers, one ruling as Sultan of Zanzibar and the other as Sultan of Oman. Zanzibar was a protectorate of the United Kingdom from 1890 to 1963, although in principle the hereditary sultans continued to rule. Meanwhile inland, the territory was divided between many tribes, mostly of the Bantu ethnic group. Each tribe had its own economy and social organization,[4] evolving with time and interacting with its neighbours:

> 'In place of the old myth that the African past was more or less static, or at best repetitive, we have to acknowledge a continuous process of social and political innovation, economic improvement and technical change.'[5]

When the British and Germans partitioned East Africa in 1886, Germany assumed responsibility for the land between the Indian Ocean and Lake Tanganyika, and the land took the name of that lake. A rebellion, known as the Maji Maji war, began in 1904 and was put down by 1906.[6] At the end of the First World War control of Tanganyika passed to the British, who governed it as a mandated territory, substantially through local leaders, until independence in 1961.

---

[4] See Roberts, *Tanzania before 1900*, for detailed studies of but seven tribes.
[5] Roberts, page ii.
[6] See Green, p19. *Maji* is Swahili for water. The Africans in this war, and some of *Mai Mai* militia in Congo, almost a century later, put their trust in 'magic' water that was supposed to render them bullet-proof.

In 1964 the Sultan of Zanzibar was deposed by a revolution, and later that same year Tanganyika and Zanzibar were joined to form the United Republic of Tanganyika and Zanzibar (later the United Republic of Tanzania). The first president of the Republic, Julius Nyerere had been a long-standing campaigner for democracy and independence, although his ideal of democracy was not the defeat of a minority by a majority, but the achieving of a consensus which would be beneficial to all. Hence the constitution was amended after independence to bring about what was effectively a one-party state. For some time Nyerere also promoted a philosophy of 'African socialism' known in Swahili as *ujamaa* (which might be translated 'family-hood'). In 1985, unusually for Africa, Nyerere handed the presidency to Ali Hassan Mwinyi without coercion; and since then two more presidents have been elected in multi-party elections: Benjamin Mkapa in 1995, and Jakaya Mrisho Kikwete in 2005.

From 1967 Tanzania, Kenya and Uganda cooperated within the framework of the East African Community, but this fell apart in 1977. The Community was re-established in 2000.

1.2 The Anglican Church in Tanzania

The existence of the Anglican Church in Tanzania is due to the work of both the Church Missionary Society and the Universities' Mission to Central Africa (UMCA).

The UMCA was founded in 1858, in response to appeals by David Livingstone for the evangelization of central Africa. Its first attempts at establishing a mission, on the borders of what are now Malawi and Mozambique, failed,[7] and Bishop Tozer and his party withdrew to Zanzibar, where the British governor asked them to take responsibility for a number of freed slaves.[8] This provided an opening for the society to work in the area.

CMS and other missions had already been working with freed slaves in East Africa, creating settlements in which they could live and work and be educated, and benefit from Christian teaching and worship. Those who adopted Christianity and showed the appropriate gifts could be trained for

---

[7]   Oliver, p15
[8]   Oliver, p18

evangelism or other tasks. Following routes frequented by the slave-traders, both CMS and UMCA established missions in various parts of Tanganyika; UMCA more in the south, in the area of Masasi, and on the shores of lake Nyasa, while CMS operated more in the centre and north of the country. The diocese of Zanzibar, formed in 1892, followed an anglo-catholic tradition of theology and worship, unlike its parent diocese of Mombasa. 'Some... had travelled as far as Zanzibar, and had come back with the story that an altogether different religion was practised there'.[9] Zanzibar gave birth to the diocese of Masasi in 1926, which in turn founded that of South-west Tanganyika in 1952. Consolidating the work of CMS in the interior, the diocese of Central Tanganyika was founded in 1926; and in 1927 the Church Missionary Society of Australia took special responsibility for its development.[10] By 1954 'a new church was being planted every week in Tanganyika'.[11] At this point the Bible Churchmen's Missionary Society (BCMS, renamed Crosslinks in 1992) also became involved in evangelism, leadership training and other work in the diocese of Central Tanganyika.

The Anglican Province of East Africa was created in 1960, and was then divided in 1970 into the Province of Kenya, and the Province of Tanzania, now renamed the Anglican Church of Tanzania. At that time there were eight Tanzanian dioceses: Zanzibar with three offspring, and Central Tanganyika with three offspring. Over subsequent decades the church grew in numbers and in its geographical coverage of the country. As new churches were planted, and new dioceses were created, they remained loyal to the traditions of their founders - the Central Tanganyika family of dioceses being evangelical Anglican and the Zanzibar family being anglo-catholic.

It is said that Anglicans travelling in the dioceses of the opposite tradition would not worship in the Anglican churches there, but availed themselves of the Lutheran or Roman Catholic churches, as appropriate. Nevertheless, in more recent years there have been a number of attempts to bring these estranged families together, as was a necessity in the very formation of a single Province of Tanzania. However, two unplanned developments were more unifying than initiatives from the top: a nation-wide acceptance of a ministry of healing, originating in the anglo-catholic Dar es Salaam from 1973; and the extension of home Bible study groups from evangelical dioceses into the coastal dioceses from the early eighties.

At the time of writing, the Anglican Church of Tanzania has 20 dioceses.

[9]   Smith, p154
[10]   *A gospel view of Tanzania* (CMSA, Sydney 2006)
[11]   Roger & Wendy Bowen, *This is your life* (Crosslinks, London, 1998)

1.3 Prayer books before 1995

In 1917, Bishop Frank Weston, deploring the diversity of liturgical uses in his diocese of Zanzibar, sought unity in the preparation of a new Swahili prayer book, to be employed by all in the diocese without exception. The clergy of the diocese appointed a committee, which adapted the eucharistic liturgy of 1549, 'with Rome supplying the priest's prayers'.[12] This text was approved by the Diocesan Synod, and then used the churches of the Diocese for many years. A revision of this was prepared in 1950 (as stated in the history in the 1995 book) or 1959 (according to Esther Mombo[13]), known as *Sala I,* adopted in some but not all parts of the Zanzibar family of dioceses.

Meanwhile in other parts of East Africa 1662 was still in use, whether in English or translated into Swahili. I have been shown a red hardback copy, 'revised by Committee' in 1962, copyright Church of the Province of East Africa, 1964, and published 'London SPCK 1968'. It would appear that 'revised' refers only to the polishing of the Swahili used, rather than the content, which is 1662 untouched by 1928. There are however a few omissions and alterations, for example[14]:
- the book begins with the order for Morning Prayer, since the 1662 Preface is printed at the back, and the lectionary and calendar are omitted.
- Various prayers for the Queen and the Royal Family are omitted or rewritten.
- The Nicene Creed has footnotes to explain the words 'Katholiko' and 'Apostoliko'.
- The 'Forms of Prayer to be Used at Sea' are omitted.
- In the Litany, the petition for travellers is expanded to include those who travel by air.

From 1963 there was an attempt to prepare a common liturgy for East Africa, by Anglicans together with Lutherans, Moravians, Methodists and Presbyterians. One text which contributed to these discussions was the *Liturgy for Africa* prepared at the request of the five Anglican Archbishops of Africa meeting in 1961, by the Archbishop of Uganda, Leslie Brown, and published in 1964.[15]

---

[12] Smith p290
[13] Hefling & Shattuck, p280
[14] These modifications, even if minor, show that those responsible were not slavishly following the original text, but paying some regard to the context.
[15] It was published in England as a small SPCK booklet, and is reproduced with an historical introduction and an *apparatus* in Colin Buchanan (ed.), *Modern Anglican Liturgies 1958-1968* (Oxford, 1968).

The *East Africa United Liturgy* was published in 1966, in both English and Swahili. However, negotiations for a union between the churches had failed in 1965, so the United Liturgy did not have a united church to use it. The Lutheran church adopted this as its official liturgy, but Anglicans did not make much use of it.[16]

From 1972 onwards Anglicans in Tanzania worked towards a truly 'common' prayer book. A eucharistic rite, drafted in Swahili and intended to unite the province liturgically, was first authorized in 1973, and then retouched in 1974 and 1977, after which it became normative and was published in 1979 (and reprinted at least in 1981).[17] The title on the front cover is 'Liturgia ya Kanisa la Jimbo la Tanzania' (Liturgy of the Church of the Province of Tanzania), and an inside page shows authorization from the Bishops of all nine diocesan bishops. Amongst notes 'to the minister' there is an explanation that an earlier version was trialed in the dioceses for three years, revised by the Committee for Liturgy and Theology, and approved for publication by the Standing Committee of the Province in 1977, in 'the hope that this Liturgy will be used throughout our Church'. The Committee notes that it referred to the East Africa United Liturgy, mentioned above, and texts from worldwide Anglican Church.[18]

A larger prayer book was printed in 1986: this included not only Holy Communion, but also Morning and Evening Prayer, with a lectionary and collects, and many of the services found in the 1995 book which is the subject of this present study.[19]

---

[16] Esther Mombo, 'Anglican Liturgies in East Africa' in Hefling & Shattuck, p279. Its text is printed with an introduction by Roger Bowen in Buchanan, *Modern Anglican Liturgies 1958-1968*.

[17] The initial 1973/74 text was published in an English translation with an introduction by Roger Bowen in Colin Buchanan (ed.), *Further Anglican Liturgies 1968-1975* (Grove Books, Bramcote, 1975). The revision of 1977 is shown in note form in Colin Buchanan (ed.), *Latest Anglican Liturgies 1976-1984* (Alcuin/SPCK, 1985).

[18] An English translation, printed in 1980, lacks the notes on pages 4 to 7 of the Swahili version, and shows some editing; for example, in the original the Te Deum is given as an alternative to the Gloria, and printed immediately after; but in the English translation the text of the Te Deum is at the back of the booklet.

[19] According to my sources – however, I regret that I have not been able to see a copy with my own eyes.

2. Democratic Republic of Congo

2.1 History - the last 500 years

Here too the first known Europeans to visit were Portuguese explorers, who found an established Kingdom of Kongo on the west coast, at the end of the fifteenth century. Friendly relations were established, and Franciscan missionaries planted churches. The Portuguese retained an interest in the area, but in 1884 the Berlin Conference (organized by European nations to determine their spheres of influence in Africa) defined an area called the Congo Free State. From 1885 this was under the personal sovereignty of King Leopold II of Belgium. But in response to oppressive exploitation and the resultant unrest, the Belgian parliament decided to take over the State as a Belgian colony in 1908.[20]

Independence from Belgium was granted in 1960, but this was followed by six years of political chaos and civil war. In 1966 Colonel Mobutu installed himself as President, bringing a measure of political stability. In the 1970s Mobutu initiated a programme of Africanization or 'authenticity'. This included the renaming of the country and the currency 'Zaire', the banning of suits and ties, and the nationalization of some industries.

Poor administration and corruption[21] slowed economic development, and by the late 1980s many areas were moving backwards in development terms, with buildings, roads and bridges built by the Belgian administration falling into disrepair. Many people were tired of Mobutu and his one-party state. With the ending of the cold war, it was clear that western countries would no longer support Mobutu as a supposed bastion against Communism, and there was growing pressure for multi-party democracy. In 1990 Mobutu legalized opposition parties, but cleverly called a national conference to draw up a new constitution. This conference and subsequent political wrangling dragged on for many years,

---

[20] For a detailed account of Leopold's rule, see Hochschild
[21] Two kinds of corrupt practice were particularly common: the favouring of members of one's own tribe or family; and the diversion of public funds.

with Mobutu exploiting the opposition's lack of unity to maximum effect. Meanwhile the annual inflation rate reached 6000% and outbreaks of military and civil unrest were common.

In October 1996 a revolution began in the east, ostensibly sparked by government oppression of the Banyamulenge people whose ancestors had migrated from Rwanda around 200 years before. They were cousins of the Tutsi, who had recently taken power in Rwanda, while Mobutu was sympathetic to the other Rwandan group, the Hutus. What appeared to begin as a Banyamulenge revolution supported by Rwanda, turned into a large-scale liberation war openly supported by the governments of Uganda, Rwanda, Burundi, and Angola, and with the sympathy of Tanzania, South Africa, and a number of western powers. The leader of the Alliance of Democratic Forces for the Liberation of Congo-Zaire was an old political opponent of Mobutu from the southern province of Katanga, one Laurent Kabila. His troops were well trained, well-equipped, and well-motivated, and by the end of May 1997 had taken over the whole country. Kabila restored the pre-Mobutu conventions, including the flag, the name of the country, and the national anthem.[22]

However, a new civil war began in August 1998, as a result of both internal disappointment with Kabila's slow delivery of promised economic improvement and democratic freedoms; and disappointment on the part of Uganda and Rwanda that incursions by their own rebels, conveniently based in Congo, had continued, and that Kabila and allied himself with the South African Development Community instead of the East African equivalent.[23]

One third of Congo was soon under the control of rival rebel movements supported by Rwanda and Uganda, while Kabila was supported by the governments of Zimbabwe, Angola and Namibia. For some years little progress was made either on the battlefront, or at the negotiating table, while many died, more from lack of food or healthcare than from the fighting itself: a study published in the medical journal *The Lancet* suggests that 'about 3·9 million people...died as a result of the conflict between August, 1998, and April, 2004'.[24]

[22] For the latter days of Mobutu's rule, see Wrong.
[23] For detailed analysis of the war, see Clark, 2002.
[24] Coghlan, Brennan, Ngoy, Dofara, Otto, Clements, & Stewart, 'Mortality in the Democratic Republic of Congo: a nationwide survey' in *The Lancet* - Vol. 367, 7 January 2006, p49

Laurent Kabila was assassinated on 16 January 2001, and his son Joseph took power. Peace talks involving several neighbouring countries and western powers eventually led to a national referendum late in 2005, and multi-party elections on 30 July 2006.

2.2 The Anglican Church in Congo

The Anglican Church came into Congo from Uganda at the end of the nineteenth century. At that time the village of Boga, located to the west of the rift valley which runs south from Lake Albert, was technically just within the British sphere of influence. The chief there asked for an evangelist to be sent to teach his people the new religion.[25] In 1896 one Apolo Kivebulaya, a Christian of the Baganda tribe, went to Boga and established a church there. He stayed for only a year, but revisited the village from time to time. He was ordained deacon in 1900, and priest in 1903. In 1915 the border was changed by agreement between the British and Belgian governments, so that the Boga area was counted as part of Congo. Apolo took up residence at Boga again in 1916 and remained there until he died in 1933, establishing numerous churches and several schools in the area. After his death, CMS missionaries were sent to Boga to continue his work. The church grew in strength and numbers, and local clergy were ordained; however the Anglican Church did not increase its geographical extent, as it was subject to 'comity' arrangements between the missionary societies.[26]

At the time of independence in 1960, the missionaries at Boga left, as did those of many other denominations. The new constitution afforded freedom of religion and worship to all in the country. The Anglican Church no longer felt bound by the old comity arrangements, and started to expand geographically, first to Bunia, the nearest large town, and then to other places along the eastern border where there were Anglicans who had migrated from Boga, from Uganda or from Rwanda.

[25] In the eyes of the uninitiated, the new religion and literacy were all part of a whole: in Swahili (and other African languages) the same verb is used for read, study, and church worship. For the implications of this, see Taylor, chapter 1

[26] According to Slade, as early as 1909, the SPG appealed for funds to establish an Anglican Chaplain in Katanga Province in the south of Congo; however 'the public was not enthusiastic... finally an arrangement was made with the Universities' Mission to Central Africa whereby an Anglican priest from the Diocese of Northern Rhodesia was periodically to visit Elisabethville' (the old name for Lubumbashi). Similar cross-border help is recorded in the mid-1950s when Anglicans who had migrated from Zambia into southern Congo formed a worshipping congregation served by a priest commuting from Ndola.

In 1972 the diocese of Boga was created, with a missionary, Philip Ridsdale, as the first bishop. Philip encouraged the expansion of the church, and welcomed 'refugee' members of other denominations which had not been able to register with the umbrella body 'Church of Christ in Zaire' and so been declared illegal.[27] The Anglican Church was attractive to others for a number of reasons:

- firm but not rigid pastoral discipline
- prevalently indigenous leadership;
- membership in a world-wide communion.

More dioceses were opened as the number of congregations grew,[28] new dioceses were formed, and the Anglican *Province* of Congo came into existence in 1992. At the time of writing there are seven dioceses. Throughout this period there was a steady increase in the number of mission partners from the UK, alongside a number from CMS Australia, and a few from the United States. Some indigenous clergy were able to study outside the country, many in Uganda, but also in Tanzania, Kenya, Britain, Canada, and the Central African Republic. A degree-level theological college, *Institut Supérieur Théologique Anglican* (ISThA), was set up to serve the whole country, functioning in Bukavu from 1981 to 1987, in Bunia from 1988 to 2003, then moving to Aru because of the second civil war.[29]

2.3 Prayer books before 1998

In places where tribes straddled the borders of Congo, many congregations benefited from prayer books translated in neighbouring countries. In the Diocese of Boga, for example, there were books from Uganda in Kihema (Kitoro), Alur[30], Lugbara[31] and Kakwa[32]. All these books had substantial collections of hymns as the second half of the book.[33]

---

[27] The Archdeaconry of Kindu, for example, was made up almost entirely of members of the *Communauté Libre de Maniema Kivu*.

[28] Diocese of Bukavu 1976; Kisangani 1980; Shaba 1986 (renamed Katanga, after the liberation war); North Kivu 1992; Kindu 1997, Kinshasa 2004, Aru 2005.

[29] It is planned to move back to Bunia as soon as the security situation has stabilized.

[30] translated by AIM missionary Seton Maclure (according to a letter from his fellow missionary, Joy Grindey, 10 April 1999).

[31] 1980 Seton MacLure (*ibid.*)

[32] 1982 Canon John Dronyi & Joy Grindey (*ibid.*)

[33] The Lugbara book contains most of the services found in the BCP, whereas the Kakwa book has only Morning Prayer, Collects and Lections, Holy Communion, Baptism of Adults, Baptism of Children, Confirmation, Holy Matrimony, and Burial of the Dead.

The Alur book was out of print when I arrived in Zaire/Congo in 1988, and the clergy serving the 20 plus Alur congregations in our area asked me what could be done about it. I suggested that we prepare a booklet with Alur versions of the most commonly used services from the Swahili book in use in Congo, and this we did: Morning/Evening Prayer, Holy Communion, Baptism, and the Marriage service. Not knowing Alur, my main contribution was as fund-raiser and technical facilitator. However, because baptisms often involved both adults and children at the same time, we merged the two baptism services in the Swahili book producing a single text for translation into Alur.

To cater for those congregations made up of people from more than one tribe, and for those tribes who had no prayer book in their own language, it had been long seen as important to make liturgy available in the Congo form of Swahili. Initially the church used services translated from English on duplicated sheets. The first prayer book of which I am aware was produced in 1973, and reprinted in 1979: Morning and Evening Prayer, Collects and Readings (references only), Holy Communion, Baptism of Children, Baptism of Adults, Catechism, Confirmation.

There then came the 1984 Prayer Book, which was much more comprehensive: Morning and Evening Prayer, Litany, Collects and Readings (in full), Holy Communion, Catechism, Baptism of Children, Baptism of Adults, Confirmation, Marriage, Burial of Adults, Burial of Children, Commissioning of Ministers, Thanksgiving. Texts had been revised, and the book was better produced than its predecessor, having rubrics in italics, and clearer print. Nevertheless, there were numerous typographical and grammatical errors. Hymns were not included in this Prayer Book because a separate collection of Swahili hymns,[34] jointly prepared by a number of protestant denominations, was available.

In 1992, at the first meeting of the Provincial Synod, immediately after the inauguration of the Province, there were two proposals:
- that the 1984 Prayer Book, of which stocks had recently run out, be reprinted immediately;
- that a completely new Prayer Book be prepared.

---

[34] *Nyimbo za Mungu.* I have seen a number of different editions; when we arrived in Zaire/Congo in 1988, most people were using a two part work, *Nyimbo za Mungu & Nyimbo za kuabudu* (Songs of God & Songs of Worship); but we purchased a newer edition in which the hymns from the second part had been intermixed with the first part, so that two different numbers had to be announced for the same hymn.

After some discussion it was agreed that the 1984 book be reprinted as soon as possible, but with corrections to the most used services, and that preparations would begin for a completely new Prayer Book to be ready in time for the Centenary of the Anglican Church in the country, in 1996.

The Synod entrusted the corrections to the diocese of Boga, and there the bishop asked me to prepare a draft. Working with a copy of the 1984 book which had already been corrected by a small committee in Boga, and incorporating further corrections, I prepared texts for Morning Prayer, Holy Communion and Thanksgiving. A small committee met in Bunia in July 1992, and, working from my drafts, fairly quickly agreed versions not just for those texts, but also for Baptism services.[35]

The texts were sent to Uzima Press in Nairobi in September 1992, but, because of lack of funds, and technical problems at the Press, the first copies were not printed until early in 1994. Meanwhile, work had begun on the more definitive new book.

---

[35] As I recall, Archbishop Njojo (who was also Bishop of Boga), Canon Diani Baguma (Dean of Boga Cathedral), Revd Isingoma Kahwa (on the staff of the theological Institute, now Bishop of Katanga), Canon Munege Kabarole (Archdeacon of Bunia) and Revd Buleta Katara (Diocesan TEE leader, and Bishop's Chaplain), and myself.

3. The 1995 prayer book of Tanzania

In Tanzania in the late 1980s the Provincial Synod established a national committee of five: Charles Mwaigoga (Bishop of South West Tanganyika), Donald Mtetemela (then Bishop of Ruaha, now the Archbishop of Tanzania), Simon Chiwanga (then General Secretary of the Province, now Bishop of Mpwapwa), Rev. Dr. H. Mtingele (later General Secretary of the Province, now General Secretary for the Bible Society of Tanzania), and Rev. John Simalenga (now Principal of St. Marks Theological College, Dar-es-Salaam). Each of these worked with a drafting group, composed mainly of Synod members, which prepared or revised separate sections of the book, mostly in the years 1988 to 1990.

The national committee revised these drafts from different groups, and they were then proof-read by the General Secretary of the Anglican Church of Tanzania, before being sent to the Provincial Synod for final approval in 1992. Page vi of the book lists all 16 bishops in office at the time of publication[36], under the words 'This Book of Prayer of the Church of the Province of Tanzania has authority to serve in our dioceses'. However, when the texts were approved it was noted that not all the material in the book would be acceptable in every diocese, and that the diocesan bishops would have discretion to direct their clergy in this regard.[37] The final part of the introduction to the book is worth translating into English, as it reflects both the tensions and the mutual respect, under God, between the two families of Tanzanian dioceses:

> 'The authorization of the Services in this book of Prayer is a very important step in the life of our Province. This book has taken into account an inheritance of customs of both sections of the Anglican church and the development of the worldwide Anglican Communion. It should be remembered that worship is offered to God, and we bring ourselves before him that we may be united with him, and that he may unite us with each other. All participate in

---

[36] The list matches that in *Crockford's* 1995-1996, i.e. those in office at the time of publication, rather than that of 1993-1994.

[37] Some bishops, even in the low church dioceses, have not exercised this discretion.

worship, and nobody is merely an actor, a watcher or a listener. With reverence and much love let us worship God, rather than follow our own practices or wishes. Even so these Services make use of human words. Shortcomings will not be absent. Hence these Services have been authorized in faith that they will help, firstly, to enhance our unity as we worship God in spirit and in truth; and second, to raise our thinking to enable the preparation of these or other services that will be even better, as we ask God in the word of the psalmist: May the words of my mouth, and the thoughts of our heart, be acceptable in your sight, O God, my rock and my Saviour.'

Representatives from Tanzania, Bishop Mdimi Mhogolo and Revd John Simalenga attended the liturgical consultation held at Kanamai in Kenya in 1993 by the Council of Anglican Provinces in Africa.[38], and shared some of their experience there, but this was too late to have a significant influence on the revision process in Tanzania. The production process began soon after, and the Book was duly authorized from 1995. The eucharistic prayer from the communion service is printed in Appendix 2 below.

42,000 copies have been sold, and are in use throughout the Province, although it is almost inevitable that in some areas older books are still in use.

---

[38] See the full report and Statement edited by David Gitari (details in bibliography).

4. The 1998 prayer book of Congo

4.1 Principles and influences

Around the same time as the Tanzanian book was being finalized, I drafted a letter from the Boga liturgical committee to the bishops of the other dioceses, outlining principles for the preparation of the new Congo book. The committee was to have discussed this letter after the September 1992 Diocesan Synod in Boga; but time was short, we did not meet, and the letter was not sent. However, the following principles were discussed informally with Synod members and theological students, without dissent being heard:

(a) The provision of alternative texts within services, for example, alternative intercessions and eucharistic prayers.

(b) Differentiation between mandatory and optional material (in the 1984 book just about everything was presumed mandatory, but, when circumstances forced pastors to abbreviate, they would cut out sections of a service - and not always the ones that I would expect!).

(c) To remember the needs and customs of African people. Here I needed to quote Article 34, and various Lambeth resolutions to show that what I proposed was not disloyal to Anglicanism.[39]   I was concerned about both style and content:
- style: that congregational responses should break up ministerial monologues, to draw people into the liturgy; and where possible to use imagery that would resonate with people's experience.
- content: that the people might pray about their real concerns, e.g. their harvest, or the bride-price at a wedding.

(d) Inclusion of services missing from the 1984 book, in particular: ordination, and the installation of an incumbent.

(e) Provision of a new lectionary to replace the two-year JLG/ASB lectionary.

---

[39] See, e.g., Resolutions 24 and 47 of the 1988 Lambeth Conference. The IALC York Statement, 'Down to Earth Worship', stemmed from Resolution 47 – see David R.Holeton (ed), *Liturgical Inculturation in the Anglican Communion* (Alcuin/GROW Joint Liturgical Study no.15, Grove Books, Bramcote, 1990)

I raised the question of whether we should be working towards one big book, or two smaller books, one with material that every Christian would want to use or refer to frequently, and another with more esoteric material. Here the consensus seemed to be that **every** Christian should be fully equipped with the **whole** liturgy of the Church - **one** book!

As I worked on the project, I took on board another principle: that the book should be a working manual for remote pastors, a source of teaching to back up the worship, and with complete rubrics governing the use of the services. In this I was influenced from two directions:

- the 1989 Prayer Book of the Church of the Province of Southern Africa, which included a page of didactic text before each service;
- the work of George Patterson in Honduras, who (albeit with a different ecclesiology) had set up a network of churches following the three-selfs principle, integrating a form of Theological Education by Extension with a strategy for church growth. His key resource was a series of 'how to...' booklets covering most aspects of church life. Church leaders were to train new church leaders on-the-job, as they opened and served new congregations.[40]

On behalf of the Province, the Archdeacon of Bunia, Canon Munege Kabarole, and I attended the Kanamai consultation in 1993, and were greatly encouraged by it. This probably influenced us in ways which I do not now recall, but it inspired me to lead a three-day seminar at ISThA on liturgy and liturgical reform in March 1994. This was helpful in three ways:

- It gave opportunity to gauge the attitude of the students to change;
- There was contact with individuals who were particularly interested in the reform process;
- Some of the small group work produced outlines for services on which later drafting was based.

4.2 Drafting

After this seminar, over the next few months I worked on the ordination services, the installation service, and the marriage service. Drafts were sent

---

[40] See George Patterson, 'Extension education for church multiplication' in Hedlund, R.E. (ed), *Church growth in the third world* (Gospel literature service, 1977); also 'Spontaneous multiplication of churches' in Winter, R.D., & Hawthorne, S. (eds), *Perspectives on the world Christian Movement* (World Christian Library, 1981). The second article is less detailed, but perhaps a more mature reflection on his work. More recent information can be found at www.trainandmultiply.info

out to the Bishops, the now-graduated ISThA students, and other interested individuals.

The Provincial Synod met in February '95, and liturgy was on the agenda.

- Delegates expressed approval of the drafts already prepared, and I was encouraged to continue in the work; however it was agreed that a conference would be needed to confirm the final texts for the new book.[41]
- A question about 'you/us' in the absolution was referred to the Synod by the group which had met to correct the 1984 Prayer Book in July 1992. This was discussed with some heat, but it was agreed in the end to allow presbyters freedom of choice.
- One bishop was anxious about the practice of baptism by immersion, which, although allowed for in the appropriate rubric of the existing prayer book, was not part of his experience of Anglicanism. I argued that baptism by immersion was a long-standing part of Christian tradition, permitted in many other provinces (even if not regularly practised); and it would be a grave mistake for the Anglican Church in Congo to cut itself off from that tradition.[42]
- The joint meeting of the Primates and Anglican Consultative Council which took place in Johannesburg in January 1993 had commended the Revised Common Lectionary for study by the provinces of the Anglican Communion, and it looked as though a number of provinces would adopt it.[43] The Synod agreed that we adopt RCL for the new book.
- I suggested omitting the Catechism from the book, but the Synod resolved that it should be retained; and requested the inclusion of the 39 Articles (so far not translated into Congo-Swahili).
- The Synod asked for the inclusion of advice on vestments, but not regulations imposing uniformity.

More services were drafted over the next two years, and some were redrafted in the light of feedback from correspondents.

---

[41] There was a suggestion that, rather than hold a conference, I visit each diocese in turn to discuss the texts, but I pointed out that this would not allow for the reconciliation of different points of view: what I agreed with diocese A might be amended by diocese B, and further amended by C, such that it was no longer recognizable by A!

[42] As I recall, no decision was taken over the issue.

[43] Although it did not fulfil all my initial criteria for a new lectionary, I could see two advantages in adopting RCL: the forging of a bond with Anglican and non-Anglican Churches around the world, and a reduction in the amount of creative new work that would have to be done.

Overall, I was disappointed with the low number of letters received in response to my drafts - often out of twenty people only two would respond. However, with the draft for the new eucharist I enclosed a user-friendly questionnaire, and this drew a relatively encouraging seven replies.

4.3 Prayer Book Workshop, Bukavu 1997

Originally planned for November 1996, the workshop was delayed partly because the drafting was not complete, and partly because of the liberation war. The workshop was held in a Roman Catholic retreat centre in Bukavu, a location chosen to minimize accommodation and transport costs.[44] Each of the six dioceses was invited to send three delegates: all but one sent their bishop as a delegate. Provincial delegates were the Provincial Secretary, the Principal of ISThA, and myself.[45]

The two-week programme gave us time for a full day on each of the major sections of the book. In many cases we were able to hold a dress-rehearsal of the proposed service, before discussing the text in detail. Although initially a few delegates felt some unease about 'play-acting' worship, we found that following orders of service through from start to finish, as though we taking part in a real service, raised many issues which would otherwise have been ignored. The workshop considered not only the texts in the book, but also the use of the texts, including linked pastoral issues, such as godparents, and how best to train worship leaders.

While some delegates had experienced the diversity of Anglican worship and teaching beyond their own dioceses, others had not. Towards the beginning of the workshop the Archbishop quoted a proverb 'He who never travels, thinks his mother is the only cook.'[46] Many had their horizons broadened by the workshop, so that by the end they were no longer asking, 'What is the right way?' but 'What is the best way for us?' Reluctance to tamper with received texts gave way to enthusiasm for creativity, and it began to appear that the rising generation of church leaders would do exciting things in the future. However there was still a good deal of discussion as to how much diversity could be allowed within the Province.[47] But we ended, for example, with three differing eucharistic prayers, printed here in Appendix2 below.

---

[44] The meeting was financed by the grants programme of Trinity Church New York.
[45] There were four observers from the Diocese of Bukavu, and three from the Province of Rwanda, all of whom contributed to the discussions but were not able to vote.
[46] A proverb also quoted by Taylor, p26, and attributed to the Baganda.
[47] As the Bishop of Bukavu said at the end of the workshop: 'When Canon Ian said that we would need to meet for two weeks to do this work, most of us thought that we would easily finish within the time; but now we have seen that there was so much to discuss that we should have planned for three weeks!'

There were three significant additions made to the list of contents in the course of the Workshop, at the request of the delegates:

- The inclusion of an order for Ministry to the Sick was proposed during the Bukavu workshop, and the text was prepared without delay. Representatives from Bukavu Diocese shared with us their locally prepared liturgy. The structure was written on the blackboard, discussed and modified. Individuals were asked to write or rewrite particular elements during a tea-break, and the whole text was later reviewed, amended and approved. The text assumes that if a presbyter is present there will be a Eucharist, and a short eucharistic prayer is included, in essence the epiclesis, narrative of institution and acclamations lifted from the first eucharistic prayer of the Communion service.[48]
- An order for the opening of a new church: I had only gone so far as to include a collect, sentences and readings, but the participants wanted more guidance as to the conduct of such a service.
- The Athanasian Creed. Some thought that this should be included since it is referred to in the 39 Articles; a few were enthusiastic about using it liturgically. Many, when they looked at the text itself, had reservations about a theology of salvation by works apparent towards the end. After some discussion, it was agreed to include the text in the book, but to add a footnote to the penultimate section, referring the reader to biblical passages assuring the salvation of those who believe.

In spite of my hopes to make the Prayer Book a self-sufficient resource for church leaders, it became apparent on the first or second day of the Workshop that there was demand for more material to be made available to ministers and theological students than we could reasonably fit into the book itself.[49] It was therefore agreed to prepare a companion booklet, and from time to time during the Workshop we would say, 'put that in the manual'.

[48] Initially I was very pleased with this co-operative effort to produce an order of service in an afternoon - I was encouraged that in ten years time, or whenever the Province again revises the liturgy, there will be energy and the creativity to do it without an outsider. However, when I got home and looked again at the minimal eucharistic prayer, which is somewhat short on *thanksgiving,* and then I remembered that it was not uncommon in our diocese at least for the consecrated bread and wine to be taken to the sick after the service, and we had made no mention of that, I appreciated the value of writing a text, circulating it, and then looking at it again a few months later! We could have done better on this one. I tried to make partial amends when I wrote the appropriate section of the manual for pastors.

[49] For example a eucharistic outline from the Dublin IALC, and the history of the practice of Confirmation.

The first draft of the manual was prepared in May 1998 for circulation to all participants of the Workshop, and others, for comment. The title was 'In spirit and in truth'. The intention was to print more than enough copies of a revised text for all the presbyters in Congo, but the civil war interrupted the printing and distribution. The book itself was printed later in 1998 in 6,500 copies at the time of the outbreak of the civil war that followed the liberation war. The division of the country between government and rebel groups made distribution of the book and training of its users very difficult, and one of the tasks for the church once the country has settled down again will be to review how widely and how well the book is being used.

5. The Contents of the Books – A Mutual Comparison

The books of both provinces are softback, and both slightly smaller than A5. The Congo book has a cover of durable blue card, and has larger pages than the Tanzanian book, although fewer of them. The Tanzanian book boasts a green cover, of card reinforced with a loose weave of fibres. The Congo book has slightly larger print, with bold headings; the Tanzanian book has more white space.

5.1 Language issues

Swahili is the language of the east African coast, combining elements of African (Bantu) languages with Arabic. It was first written down using Arabic script, but when missionaries arrived in the 19th century, they wrote Swahili using the Latin alphabet. Swahili was taken inland initially by traders, including slave-traders, and later by missionaries and agents of the European powers active in eastern Africa in the 19th and 20th centuries. While there is no doubt that Swahili is an indigenous language, missionaries and educationalists have influenced its development over the last hundred years, making it more regular, and easier to learn. Although there are households where Swahili is the first language that children learn, Swahili is most often a second language.

In Tanzania Swahili has the status of National Language and is the main language used for church services and church business. Swahili is the first language of literacy, but often the second language of speech. In the Democratic Republic of Congo, French is the 'Official Language', and Swahili is one of four regional languages referred to as 'National Languages'. The Anglican Church, first planted in a Swahili region, uses Swahili for most official purposes, but also uses other languages where appropriate. It is not unusual to attend a service where two languages are used.

Congo-Swahili[50] is slightly different from the 'Standard' Swahili used in Tanzania[51] and Kenya, both in grammar and vocabulary, but on the whole the two languages are mutually intelligible. Some common features that should be remembered as we look at the two books:

---

[50] Sometimes called *kingwana*, and sometimes considered an inferior form of language, even by its own speakers. Standardization of the grammar has often been the work of the churches.
[51] Where the development of the language is controlled by the Institute of Swahili Research (TUKI) in the University of Dar es Salaam.

- There is no distinction between masculine and feminine pronouns: ie 'he', 'she' and 'it' are all one word.
- Swahili has two words for priest:
  kuhani - Old Testament priest
  kasisi – New Testament presbyter (still regularly called a 'priest' in English-language Anglicanism).
  To reflect this distinction, when translating Swahili into English, I have consistently used 'presbyter' for *kasisi*.
- It usual in Swahili to write rubrics in the subjunctive; in English it is usual to employ the present tense.

There are significant differences between the languages.
- The most obvious grammatical difference is that the noun classes with the prefix *m-* in Standard Swahili have the prefix *mu-* in Congo Swahili.[52]
- Standard Swahili has more loan words from Arabic - for example, the multiples of ten, while Congo Swahili says 'two tens' etc.
- The words for the days of the week in Standard Swahili hinge around the Muslim special day of Friday, *Ijumaa*. The words for Saturday through to Wednesday are based on the numbers one to five. So Sunday is often refered to as *jumapili* (second day), though Christians sometimes call Sunday, *Siku ya Bwana* (Day of the Lord). Within T1995 both terms are used. In Congo-Swahili the days from Monday to Saturday are described as 'first day' etc. For Sunday the French name, *Dimanche*, is sometimes used; as is *Siku ya Yenga* (Day of Rest), and *Siku ya Mungu* (Day of God). After discussion, it was agreed to use the latter in C1998.
- In Congo Swahili less use is made of abstract nouns, adverbs or adjectives: to be comprehensible to the greatest number, it is best to explain a concept by using a phrase rather than a single word that many people may find obscure.
- There are probably more local variations in Swahili grammar and vocabulary within Congo, than within Tanzania. We chose to follow the usage in a recent Congo-Swahili translation of the Bible.[53]

---

[52] For example, *mtu* (man) becomes *mutu*, and *mti* (tree) becomes *muti*.
[53] A particular issue of debate was which form of the possessive to use with 'Father' (*Baba*) and 'Lord' (*Bwana*).

5.2 Cultural issues

Different people groups live and think in diverse ways. If we see liturgy is a means of communication between changeless God and diverse humanity, then liturgy needs to be suited to the people who are using it. This is not just about translating the words into the language of a particular group, but shaping the liturgy to engage with their particular concerns and way of thinking. The 34th of the 39 Articles of Religion states:

> 'It is not necessary that Traditions and Ceremonies be in all places one, or utterly like; for at all times they have been divers, and may be changed according to the diversities of countries, times, and men's manners, so that nothing be ordained against God's Word.'

Others have discussed the principles of 'inculturation' at length, and there is no need to rehearse them here. However, inculturation is easier said than done. In any country composed of many different tribes, each with its own language and traditions, how can anyone incorporate local cultural elements from one without offending members of other tribes? Careful choice of imagery is important.[54] There are also significant cultural variations between urban life and rural life.

Nevertheless common themes and concerns may be discerned. For example, a study by Wood and Wild-Wood of the songs used in Anglican churches in north-east Congo[55] brings out particular theological emphases, even though people of several tribes were involved. Some of these relate to concepts in traditional African spirituality, others may be a legacy from nineteenth-century missionary beliefs and attitudes. Wood and Wild-Wood's study is to be commended because they analysed the repertoire of songs that the people choose to sing, as opposed to the complete text of the hymn book.

It is difficult for outsiders to grasp what is really going on in a situation. Sometimes for reasons of politeness, an informant will give a researcher the answer that the informant thinks the researcher wants to hear, or that the informant's bishop would want him to give.[56]

---

[54] For example, in European culture the owl is a symbol of wisdom, whereas in many African cultures the owl is a symbol of bad luck or death. Consider also Buchanan in Alcuin/GROW 28, p10

[55] Wood,Peter, Wild-Wood, Emma, *One day we will sing in God's home: Hymns and songs sung in the Anglican Church in North-East Congo (DRC)*, Journal of Religion in Africa, 34, 1, 3/1/2004, pp 145-180

[56] Maia Green, coming to Tanzania as a secular researcher, may have had some advantage over Christian scholars. Among other interesting observations she suggests that a traditional African concept of blessing (*baraka*) determined the way in which the people of southern Tanzania understood Christianity.

Wood and Wild-Wood also remind us that 'liturgy is not to be confused with the official text'. [57] The words in the book may take up only a small proportion of the duration of the service. Much of the local culture is often reflected in the choice of congregational and choir songs, the layout of the church, the content and style of notices, the clothing of leaders and participants, etc. The Roman Catholic Church in Congo is noted for its Africanized Mass[58]. When I asked my local Jesuit priests for the text, I was told. 'It is not the text, it is the way we do it.'

So, in looking at these two prayer books, we shall watch for evidence that they were prepared for use in Africa, rather than elsewhere.

5.3 Morning and evening prayer

Due to the ratio of presbyters to churches in both countries, Morning Prayer would be the norm on most Sundays in a typical rural church. The two books provide for these offices in different ways; this table shows the contents of each book, in the order printed.

Tanzania 1995	Congo 1998
Morning Prayer; ten canticles are printed within the order.	**Morning prayer**, with signs to show which sections may be omitted other than in the principle Sunday service; canticles for different seasons or days are indicated but not printed.
Shorter form of Morning Prayer; three canticles are printed in the order.	
	Canticles - eleven provided for use either morning or evening.
Evening Prayer; with three canticles printed.	**Evening prayer**, with signs to show which sections may be omitted other than in the principal Sunday service; canticles for different seasons or days are indicated but not printed.
Shorter form of Evening Prayer; two canticles are printed in the order.	
Prayers and thanksgivings for each day of the week, morning and evening	
Night Prayer; with six canticles.	

---

[57] Colin Buchanan in Alcuin/GROW 28, p17
[58] This is sometimes known as the Zaire Mass, recalling the pre-liberation name of the country. See Tovey, p126-p129

The Canticles provided in C1998 are (# = metrical setting with tune in solfa notation provided): Venite; Te Deum; Jubilate; Benedicite; Gloria#; Magnificat#; Song of the Holy Spirit#; Nunc#; Easter Anthems#; Benedictus.[59] T1995 offers a greater variety of canticles, but none of them is given a tune.

In more detail, we can compare the orders for Morning Prayer.

Tanzania	Congo
'In the name of the Father...'	[+] Verse of the day, [+] Statement of purpose
Scripture verses & Ps 51.15 as V&R[60]	Ps 51.15 as V&R & seasonal responses
°Penitence	Canticle (by day of week or season)
Ps 70:1 as V&R & Gloria patri	
Venite	Penitence
Psalm of the day	[+] Psalm of the day
Reading (OT, if long form) [+] Reading (OT)	
Canticle (by day of week)	[+] Canticle (by season)
°Reading (NT)	Reading (NT)
°Sermon	Sermon
Canticle: Benedictus or Jubilate	
°Apostles Creed	[+] Apostles Creed
Collect of the day Prayers & thanksgivings (by day of week) Prayers for peace and grace Lord's Prayer Prayer of Chrysostom	Threefold kyrie Lord's Prayer [+] Responsory (cp 1662) Collect of the day Prayers for peace and [+] grace [+] Intercessions Prayer of Chrysostom
Blessing, or grace or dismissal responsory	Blessing or Grace

Note: The ° symbol in T1995 shows what may be omitted to form the shorter Morning Prayer, which is printed separately: the [+] symbol in Z1998 shows what may be omitted when the service is not a principal Sunday service.

[59]   Sources of tunes: for the Gloria, a setting pioneered by the choir of Bukavu cathedral, but also used in other dioceses; for the Magnificat, two settings, one already in use by ecumenical women's groups in the Bukavu area, and the other to the tune of a Kenyan pop song, *Jambo, jambo bwana*; the Song of the Holy Spirit was composed as a song by the catechist Samson Ozua in Aru; the Nunc Dimittis was set to the tune used for the hymn 'Precious blood of Jesus'; and the Easter Anthems were set to the tune of the hymn 'Earthly pleasures vainly call me'.

[60]   as Versicle and Response

Comparing the longer forms of the service in the two books we note that while there are many similarities, there are a few significant differences:
- T1995 has three canticles, while C1998 has only two;
- the penitential section and the first canticle are in a different order; Congo was here following the example of Southern Africa.
- C1998 gives greater variety of canticle usage (more so given that the rubrics only suggest which canticle to use, rather than dictate);
- the prayers and thanksgivings for different days of the week are unique to T1995 - more on this below;
- the optional dismissal responsary[61] in T1995 is of high church origin, and controversial for others, as it implies that the dead need our prayers.

Comparing the shorter forms of the service, we note that Congo was unwilling to dispense with either penitence or sermon.

The daily prayers and thanksgivings used in T1995 are worth noting as they do not have parallels elsewhere. They all take the same form[62], but with two intentions for each office.

	Morning	Evening
Sun	- that the Church stand firm. - that people turn to Christ.	- thanks for God's kindness. - thanks for the gifts of the Spirit
Mon	- for the United Nations - all in authority	- our Bishop - the Ministers of the Church
Tues	- all who are taught the faith - all who teach the faith	- thanks for our salvation - thanks for all who help the work of the Church
Weds	- for the Church's peace and unity - that all who dwell in sin repent	- those preparing for ordination - those preparing for confirmation
Thur	- that God increase our mutual love - that God bring peace to the world	- thanks for the spread of the Gospel - those preparing for baptism
Fri	- that God bless our work - for all humanity	- those who hear the Word - thank God for the protection of the Holy Angels
Sat	- vocations to the service of the church and the religious life - those who scorn the Gospel and persecute the Church	- the sick - those who live in our parishes

[61] Ending with: May the spirits of the faithful by the mercy of God rest in peace.
[62] A simple bidding from the minister, followed by a response, a versicle and another response; then a collect comprising several full lines of text, said by the minister.

5.4 Eucharist

We compare the orders for the Eucharist, in the following table, ignoring hymns.

We note some obvious contrasts:

- C1998 offers a richer diet, with a number of alternative texts; T1995 is sparse, by comparison, lacking even one Collect for Purity.
- Again, as with the Congo Morning Prayer, the [+] symbol shows what may be omitted when celebrating a eucharist which is not a principal Sunday service; helpful, for example, at a eucharist held before a business meeting of a parish or an archdeaconry. T1995 makes no provision for a shorter service.
- T1995 has the Lord's Prayer after the eucharistic prayer, as do many other Anglican prayer books around the world; C1998, like Nigeria, has it following and rounding up the intercessions.
- T1995 on the other hand, has the peace after the preparation of the table, as in the Tanzanian orders of 1979, following the model of the 1964 *Liturgy for Africa*; while C1998 has it in the more conventional position before the preparation.

I understand that the eucharist of T1995 was hardly changed from that in T1986; apparently the 1986 eucharist was considered the best possible solution for the Province, which people were subsequently reluctant to tinker with. In Congo, however, there was enthusiasm to build on and enrich the existing provision. The eucharistic prayers of both rites are printed out in Appendix 2 below.

Tanzania	Congo
	[+] Verse of scripture set (cp ASB)
Greeting	Greeting (with Easter insert)
	[+] Collect for purity (2 options)
Summary of the Law *or* Ten Commandments (simple)	[+] Ten Commandments (inc. NT phrases) *or* Summary of the Law
Sixfold or ninefold Kyrie	
Call to repentance Confession (cp CW p169a) Absolution	Call to repentance Confession (cp CW p169a) Absolution
Gloria	[+] Gloria
Collect	Collect
Readings & Sermon	Readings & Sermon
Nicene Creed	[+] Nicene Creed

Intercessions (one form printed, others may be used)	[+] Intercessions (three forms printed)
	Lord's Prayer
Preparation of the table and the offering of gifts	[+] Sharing of the Peace (5 options for the introduction)
Sharing of the Peace (no introductory sentence)	Preparation of the table and the offering of gifts
Eucharistic prayer (8 seasonal inserts)	Eucharistic prayer (three forms, of which the first has 11 seasonal inserts)
Lord's Prayer	
Lamb of God The bread which we break V & R	
Prayer of humble access	Prayer of humble access
Distribution	Distribution
Psalm 103.1-5, 22 as responsary	Post-communion prayer (2 options, cp CW)
Post-communion prayer (cp CW short)	[+] Verse of scripture set (cp ASB)
Blessing (4 options)	[+] Blessing (with 9 seasonal alternatives)
Dismissal	Dismissal (with Easter alternative)

The three intercession options in C1998 are differently shaped:
  a) a litany with 11 short biddings, with a uniform response, 'Good Lord hear us'; optionally concluding with silent or open prayer. The litany was adapted from the latest Kenyan eucharist.
  b) a litany modelled on one from Southern Africa but recast to be more trinitarian[63], with four biddings addressed to the Father, five addressed to the Son, and three referring to the work of the Spirit: the response varying with the person of the trinity referred to.[64]
  c) an enhancement of the form in the previous book, itself based on England's Series 3.

Readers may be interested to know what eucharistic theology is implied by the liturgies, although in Congo this was less of a hot topic than I expected. T1995's eucharistic prayer asks that 'we may be partakers of his body and blood'. In Z1984 the wording was 'grant that these gifts of bread and wine may be to us his Body and his Blood'. This allows the reader to have some freedom of interpretation: in summary, is the minister

---

[63] The CPSA original (*An Anglican Prayer Book*, p113, form C) had seven petitions addressed to the Father, fifteen to the Son.
[64] An earlier draft had petitions directed to the Spirit, but some members of the Bukavu workshop were uneasy about this.

praying for a transformation of the *elements*, or of the *recipients*, or of the *relationship* between them? See Appendix 2.

In the first draft of C1998, the first eucharistic prayer retained the exact wording of the former book; in the second prayer, we replaced 'wine' with 'cup' and dropped the capitalization; and in the third prayer we restructured the petition thus: 'may this bread be to us his body, and may this wine be to us his blood'.

In response to the circulation of this draft, letters of concern came from two mission partners (CMS Australia), and two of their pupils. One of the Australians proposed 'may we be partakers of his body and blood'. When I put this to my correspondents in the second questionnaire about Holy Communion, there were three votes in favour and one against. In the draft revised for the Bukavu workshop, the new wording was adopted for the first two prayers, but the third prayer was unchanged. The first two prayers were passed without question; when the wording in the third prayer was questioned I pointed out that it afforded liberty of interpretation, and it was approved.

In the pages of teaching printed in C1998 before the rubrics and the service, the communicant is advised to reflect on one or two of the following themes when coming to Communion: repentance, the gift of eternal life, thanksgiving, obedience, the promise of the Holy Spirit, the unity of Christians world-wide. This is followed by a paragraph explaining that the body of and blood of Jesus are received in a spiritual sense.[65]

One might also note that in T1995 and C1998A, the elements are prayed about before the narrative of institution, and with no reference to the Holy Spirit; in C1998 prayers B and C, the elements are prayed over after the narrative, and with reference to the power of the Holy Spirit. It is interesting to note that in the whole written and verbal debate, nobody commented on the references to receiving Christ's body and blood in the prayer of humble access, or in the post-communion prayers.

---

[65] Through many years of church history, Christians have taught a variety of things about Holy Communion. Some have said that the bread and wine change within themselves to become the body and blood of Jesus, since Jesus said to his disciples, 'This is my body, this is my blood'. But it seems that Jesus wanted to explain a spiritual truth, in the same way as he called himself the light of the world, a shepherd, and a vine. So in this service we physically receive the bread and the wine, but spiritually, by our faith and the aid of the Holy Spirit, we increase within us the life of Jesus who died for our sake.

The penitential section in Z1994 came after the intercessions, as in Series 3. The draft of the Communion service considered at Bukavu allowed for the prayers of penitence to be there, or as a response to the preaching, or near the beginning of the service. However, the workshop agreed to anchor them to avoid confusion, and to do so at the beginning of the service as a preparation for worship.[66]

5.5 Baptism

Omitting hymns, we can compare the two main orders thus:

Tanzania (adults)	Congo
Introduction (cp 1662)	Greeting and informal introduction
	Psalm or song (Ps 34.1-8 suggested)
Prayer for the candidates (cp 1662)	Prayer for the candidates
	Readings
	Sermon *and/or* given text about baptism
	° Three questions to parents and godparents of infant candidates ° Mark 10.13-15 ° Prayer for infant candidates
Questions to candidates and sponsors: • rejection of Satan and all evil • repetition and affirmation of Apostles Creed • desire to be baptized • continued obedience to God	Four questions to candidates *and/or* parents and godparents: • turning to Christ • repenting of sin • refusing the evil of Satan and others • refusing the lusts of the body
Question to the congregation	Prayer over the water
Four short prayers for the purity and holiness of the candidates (cp 1662)	Three questions to candidates *and/or* parents and godparents, ascertaining faith and trust in the Father who created, the Son who redeems and the Holy Spirit who sanctifies; with a final congregational affirmation (cp ASB)
Prayer over the water (begins with responses like a Eucharistic prayer)	
Baptism by pouring (or submersion)	Baptism by submersion or pouring
Signing with the cross	Signing with the cross
* Robing the candidates in white	Welcome from the congregation
* Giving of a candle	Lord's Prayer
Prayer for the newly baptized	Prayer for the newly baptized
Commission for the newly baptized	Blessing or grace

*indicates optional items, 'for use where there is this custom'; and in the Congo order, ° shows those to be used at the baptism of infants.

[66] Dirokpa regrets this in his thesis (p115), and proposes that penitence should come between the Creed and the intercessions (p307).

Tanzania also has an alternative service for the baptism of infants[67], which differs from the adult service in three ways:

- the initial question, about Satan and evil, is broken into three parts, though these cover the same catalogue of evils
- before the four short prayers, the minister may 'where there is this custom' command Satan to leave the infants[68], and then sign the infants with the cross in the 'oil of salvation'.
- after the prayer for the newly baptised, the godparents are charged with the duties of teaching them all that they need to know as Christians, and bringing them to confirmation at the appropriate age. The service then concludes with the Lord's Prayer.

The order for baptism in T1995 is not intended to stand alone, but should be part of a larger service, and readings and a collect given in a rubric; however, C1998 gives an order that can stand alone, but with instructions for integrating it with Morning Prayer or Holy Communion.

In rubrics before the service, T1995 commends the use of 'much water' but counsels care; while C1998 states that baptism by pouring is the norm for the Province, but allows for baptism by immersion, if the candidate requests it, and the presbyter agrees, and the baptism can be carried out in an orderly manner, causing neither danger to health nor division in the church.

C1998 has one service which can be used for adults and/or infants. This change from earlier prayer books was mainly for the practical reason that adults and infants were often baptized together, which needed constant page-turning from one service to another. It also made the theological point that infant baptism and adult baptism are the same thing.

In T1995 the minister's introduction to the prayer for the newly baptized, adult and infant, states that they have been 'born again', and uses the term 'born again' also elsewhere in the service. C1998 is more coy on baptismal regeneration; the closest reference in the service itself being in the prayer for the baptized, which gives thanks 'that your Holy Spirit makes us your children, and also through baptism we become members[69] of your Church.' The page of teaching before the service says that 'the

---

[67] It appears to have some printing errors: the rubrics bid the minister to question the godparents, in one place with the parents, in another alone, and in another with the candidates.

[68] The text is similar to that in 1549, which is however addressed to an 'uncleane spirite'.

[69] *viungo*, literally 'limbs', drawing on New Testament body imagery.

task of baptism is to show who are members[70] of the church. Only God can see into people's hearts and recognize how many people are his.'

Both books make provision for emergency baptism of the sick, by any Christian.[71] C1998 does this by means of one of the notes before the service, which also says that there should be no signing with the cross, unless the sick person recovers and comes to church to be welcomed. T1995 offers an abbreviated order of service, comprising the Lord's Prayer, a prayer of faith and repentance to be said by an adult candidate, the baptism itself, and a slightly longer post-baptismal prayer than usual.

5.6 Confirmation

In both Congo and Tanzania, confirmation is a major event in the life of a parish. Once each year, if they are lucky, the bishop will arrive to confirm, probably staying overnight, and bringing with him guests from diocesan headquarters or from other parts of the diocese. The catechists who work in the various churches in the parish will have been preparing candidates for months in advance, and they will bring their candidates, possibly one or two days before the service, so that the incumbent of the parish may vet them and top up the teaching that they have received. Candidates may camp in a local school or other buildings made available to them, and are likely to bring their own food. To feed the bishop and other guests, the incumbent is likely to request donations of food from the various churches – a chicken from here, some bananas from there, rice or another staple from somewhere else. In the days before the bishop arrives the vegetation around the church will be manicured, paths swept, and overdue building maintenance and cleaning will be carried out.

On the big day guests from other denominations and the civil administration will be given places of honour in the church, the congregation will be swollen with the candidates' supporters, and choirs from their churches will turn up expecting to sing at least one item from their repertoire. Nobody will go home hungry. This can be a very joyful time, when the church community is seen at its best – although behind the scenes it can be a logistical nightmare! Yet, none of this cultural context is revealed in either of the prayer books that we are studying.

---

[70] *wanamemba*, a word for 'members' with no anatomical connotations.
[71] After which the incumbent of the parish should be informed as soon as possible.

Both books assume that confirmation will take place in the context of a Communion service (although T1995 does allow for it not to). The order that follows is to be included after the sermon (or the gospel in T1995):

Tanzania	Congo
	Song, psalm or responsary based on Ps 139.1-3, Ps 65.3-4, Ps 84.10-11
Incumbent presents the candidates to the bishop who asks him whether they have been taught the faith	Incumbent presents the candidates to the bishop who asks him whether they have been taught the faith. He also asks the consent of all present.
	Bishop prays (*ad* ASB p227 para 4)
Six questions including reference back to the promises made at baptism, touching on evil and living the Christian life, and ending with a recitation of the Apostles' Creed.	Four questions about turning to Christ and leaving evil (as at baptism)
	Three questions about believing and trusting in Father Son and Holy Spirit
	Six questions about the Christian life
Bishop asks all present whether they will set a good example for the newly confirmed The Bishop briefly prays for the Spirit to descend on all the candidates. A short responsary (*ad* 1662)	Optional song calling on the Spirit
Bishop prays for the candidates (*ad* 1662 – extra 'Amens' added)	Bishop prays for the candidates (*cp* 1662)
Where anointing is traditional: • Bishop prays for all the candidates • Bishops signs each with the cross and lays hands on each, with prayer Where anointing is not traditional: • Bishop lays hands on each, saying for each the 1662 prayer, 'Defend, O Lord, this your servant...'	Bishop lays hands on and prays for each: 'O Lord, give this servant of yours the strength of your Holy Spirit.' All pray for the candidates, as in ASB, the words used by Bishop alone in 1662: 'Defend O Lord, these your servants...'
After the words of the peace, the bishop prays at length for the candidates, and blesses them. (*cp* 1549)	Bishop commissions and prays for the candidates with words based on the so-called Prayer of St Francis of Assisi

(In neither book is the posture of the bishop specified at the laying on of hands)

Again we note that our two liturgies draw on varied sources, and again we see differing provision for the two traditions in Tanzania. Congo's six questions about living as a Christian were based on five questions in the baptism service of A1979, and the eleven questions in K2002's liturgy for

'Confirmation and Commissioning for Service and Witness'.[72] Most of the themes in the latter were retained, though the order was made more logical. At the Bukavu workshop a delegate asked for a reference to tribalism in the fifth question, and there was drafted an amendment using the word 'favouritism' thinking thereby to cover a wider range of sins; and though the delegates appreciated that, they insisted on naming tribalism as well, so the final version has both words.

Bishop So that all people may understand your intent to give your whole life in the service of the Lord, I ask you:
Will you persist in the study of the Word of God, living in unity with the faithful, partaking at the Lord's Table, and in prayer?
Answer I will do this with God's help.
Bishop Will you bear witness to the love of Jesus before your neighbours, in your words and deeds every day?
Answer I will do this with God's help.
Bishop Will you pray for and support the Church, its bishops, presbyters and other servants?
Answer I will do this with God's help.
Bishop Will you try to satisfy the hungry and thirsty, to care for those who have no family, and to welcome strangers?
Answer I will do this with God's help.
Bishop Will you be a faithful citizen of this country, praying for its leaders, and upholding justice, truth and peace amongst all people, without tribalism or favouritism of any kind?
Answer I will do this with God's help.
Bishop Will you be a good steward of the world God created, protecting its goodness[73]?
Answer I will do this with God's help.

Of the six questions in T1995, the first two repeat the baptismal decision, three are about the Christian life, covering similar themes to the first three questions above, and the last introduces the Apostles' Creed.

---

[72] Why six? Eleven seemed too many, and six was chosen to complement the six theological questions preceding (in an earlier draft!).
[73] The Swahili word *uzuri* can mean both goodness and beauty; it is derived from the word for good, and should remind people that 'God saw it was good'.

5.7 Marriage

Tanzania	Congo
	Either 1 John 4.16 or Jeremiah 33.11
	Opening prayer
	Readings and sermon
Preface (cp1662, omitting the 3 reasons)	Preface (ad ASB)
Congregation and couple are given the opportunity to declare impediment	Congregation and couple are given the opportunity to declare impediment
Sermon	
Bride and groom are asked to consent	Bride and groom are asked to consent
Congregation is asked to set a good example of fidelity, & give support	Congregation is asked to give support
Bride and groom are each 'brought' by their father or brother[74] or friend.	Bride and groom are each 'brought' by their father or a family member
Parallel vows are exchanged (cp ASB)	Parallel vows are exchanged
Rings are blessed and exchanged.	Rings are blessed and exchanged (with an option for only one ring).
Presbyter prays for the couple (ad 1662)	
The hands of the couple are joined, and they are proclaimed husband & wife.	They are proclaimed husband & wife, And their hands are joined.
The presbyter blesses the couple (1662)	The presbyter blesses the couple (ASB)
Psalm 128 or Psalm 67	Optional acclamations (cp ASB)
Six-fold kyrie, Lord's Prayer, respons-ary (1662), more prayers (ad 1662)	Prayers, ending with the Lord's Prayer
Collect and readings	Signing of the register
Holy Communion liturgy optional, with collect and readings provided.	Holy Communion liturgy optional
	Optional giving of gifts, and advice
Final prayer for the couple	Dismissal of couple
Signing of the register	Blessing

T1995 commends the celebration of Holy Communion with the marriage; C1998 makes provision for it but neither commends nor discourages.

It is interesting to note that in both books, both the bride and the groom are 'given' away, subverting patriarchal traditions both European and African. In Tanzania the individuals are handed to the minister with no words on the part of the giver. In Congo this dialogue is used for the groom:

---

[74] The Swahili word *ndugu* can sometimes also mean sister or cousin.

Q. Who gives this man, to be united with this woman, to begin a new life
   and to found a new household?
A. I give him; we say farewell to him with sadness, but rejoice for his sake.[75]

We were trying to convey the scriptural ideas of 'leaving and cleaving'
here[76] – it seemed that traditionally parental ties were considered stronger
than marital ties, so that parents might call one of the partners back to
help with the harvest, leaving the other literally holding the baby.

There was discussion at Bukavu about the use of traditional symbols of
marriage instead of wedding rings, as allowed by the Episcopal Church of
the USA,[77] and commended by the Consultation at Kanamai.[78] Examples
given are necklaces and bracelets. A survey around the room showed little
knowledge of durable[79] traditional symbols in use by the tribes in Congo
with which participants were familiar, but a note was agreed allowing
individual dioceses to authorize alternatives if required:
    'With the approval of the Diocese, other symbols which do not conflict
    with the Gospel, may be used in place of rings, in accordance with the
    ancient custom of the family of the man or woman.'
In T1995 the prayers after the Psalm are based on 1662, and have no
flexibility. C1998 allows the minister to use two or more of five prayers
printed, or prayers from elsewhere.

A bride-price system still operates in most parts of Congo, under which
the groom pays a substantial amount to the family of the bride. A large
part is normally paid before approval is given for a marriage in church, but
often there is still something to pay in instalments later on. The payment
of bride-price is a major issue for those getting married, and on the minds
of many others at the wedding. It therefore seemed right to include an
optional prayer on the subject:
    We thank you every day, God of eternity,
    because your love has no end,
    and we cannot count your gifts to us.[80]

---

[75] The word used for 'give' (*kutoa*) also carries connotations of sacrificial offering; the word used for
      'household' (*nyumba*) literally means 'house' but can also carry the wider meaning. The 'I' at the
      beginning of the response is emphatic.
[76] Matthew 19.5, KJV
[77] *Book of Common Prayer*, Order for Marriage, Additional directions; p437 in the pocket edition.
[78] Kanamai Statement, section 4, paragraph 4.4
[79] In some places garlands of flowers may be exchanged!
[80] As God is thanked for his generosity, perhaps those involved in the giving of the bride and the
      giving of the bride-price will be encouraged to do so in a spirit of generosity.

And today we thank you because this man has given wealth
as a sign of love and respect[81] towards the family of the woman.
Help him to increase their joy,[82]
and to build unity between these two families.[83]
In the name of our Saviour Jesus Christ. **Amen.**

5.8 At time of death

The provision for worship at the time of death is quite different in the two books.

In many parts of both Congo and Tanzania, immediately after a Christian dies, a catechist or other church leader goes to pray with the family and to encourage the faithful to sing hymns rather than mourn with the traditional loud wailing. For practical reasons, the burial normally takes place within 24 hours, the service being held at the deceased's home. In rural areas the grave is dug near to the home, on the family land; but in town a cemetery grave has become compulsory and there is a procession between the main part of the service and the interment. About a week later, but sometimes as soon as three days after the burial, a memorial service is be held. In the Boga area the memorial service would be held 90 days after the death, and would be an occasion for traditional rituals.[84]

Recognizing this pattern, C1998 has three orders of service:
- a short order to be used with the family and other mourners when a minister arrives at the home;[85]
- a burial service allowing for a procession to the grave;
- a memorial service.

T1995 however focuses on the burial, with one service for the burial of a Christian, and one for a Christian who has withdrawn from the church or committed suicide. The first of these services is intended to begin in church, preferably with Holy Communion, while the second is to be conducted at the burial ground.

We can compare the two principal orders for burial.

---

[81] It is said that bride-price should be seen as a love-gift rather than a commercial transaction.
[82] By completing any part of the bride-price still outstanding, as well as by being a good son-in-law!
[83] In many cases the groom will have been helped by father, brothers, and possibly uncles. Whether this is true or not, the marriage will be seen as a bond not just between two individuals but between two families.
[84] If the deceased was regarded as head of the extended family, the memorial service may be the time when his successor is acknowledged in some way.
[85] This is similar to that in NZ1989, p812, but with a sermon.

Tanzania	Congo
Opening verses: John 11.25f, Job 19.25-27, 1 Tim 6.7/Job 1.21	One or more opening verses[86]: John 11.25f, Rom 8.38f, Ps 25.7, 1 Tim 6.7/Job 1.21, 1 Cor 2.9
Introduction	Introduction
Psalm 39, 51 or 90	A prayer for the mourners (NZ1989)
Order for Holy Communion inserted here, with specific collect and readings	

* 'If the Bishop permits':
• A prayer for the deceased to be
  spared judgement
• Responsary, sixfold kyrie & Lord's Prayer
• Water and incense accompanied by a
  responsary for the deceased
• Prayer for safety of the deceased[87]
	* One person who knew the deceased
	  well briefly speaks of the work that
	  God did in his life
	* A prayer of thanksgiving for the
	  deceased

	Psalm 23 or 121
	Readings and sermon
	Lord's Prayer and other prayers
	* viewing the face of the deceased, while a song is sung
Procession to the grave	*Procession to the grave*
Blessing of the grave, if not in consecrated ground	Verses from scripture, or Psalm 103
As the body is put into the grave, the Benedictus is sung.	
Words of committal (1662, from 'Man that is born...)	Words of committal (ASB, from 'We have entrusted...')
Prayer for that we may be raised from the death of sin (*ad* 1662)	* Songs while the grave is filled
	Verses: Psalm 16.11, Jude 24
Grace or responsary for 'rest eternal'	Dismissal responsary including the Easter greeting

* optional

I understand from a member of the Tanzanian drafting group that it was divided over prayers for the deceased, but those against such prayers were over-ruled by a bishop of the UMCA tradition. Even so the section of the service where most of this material is found is marked 'if the bishop permits', to allow variation between dioceses.

The traditional rituals at the time of death and in the subsequent months vary greatly from tribe to tribe. One common example has been the shaving of the heads of surviving relatives, as a sign of mourning and a

[86] For a child: Rev 7.17, Isaiah 40.11, Luke 18.16, Matthew 18.10
[87] Everything in this box, and below, is taken from the Mass of the Dead in the Presence of the Body, in the Roman Catholic Tridentine Rite.

new start; another has required a widow to have sexual intercourse with a male relative of the deceased. A paragraph at the end of the teaching preceding the rubrics says this:

'...in Congo there are various customs at the time of death. Some are unacceptable to Christians, because they do not accord with the teaching of the Bible. But others may be performed in an attitude of prayer, without sin and without shame.'

The memorial service in the Congo book is designed to be very flexible, so that it can be used at any time before or after the funeral, or with people mourning somebody who has died and been buried far away.

After the three orders of service, the Congo book offers a selection of prayers for use in any of them:

A. [comfort for those mourning] a child (NZ1989)
B. a sudden death (Kanamai)
C. an unmarried adult (Kanamai)
D. a mother and father who die together (Kanamai)
E. a person with neither family nor friends nearby (South Africa)
F. for those of us who remain ('until the shadows lengthen')

The Kanamai prayer for use after a suicide was included in the draft, but was removed at Bukavu.

5.9 Thanksgivings

The Tanzanian book has two orders of service for giving thanks.

The first is an order for 'the thanksgiving of parents', to be used 'after the birth of a child', normally in church, but 'if necessary' in hospital or at home. It consists of an introduction; a Psalm (either 121 or 116); sixfold kyrie and Lord's Prayer; a responsary prayer for the salvation and protection of the mother; a prayer of thanksgiving that the mother survived childbirth, asking that she might continue in a life of faith and obedience; a prayer thanking God that the parents have been blessed with the gift of a child, and asking that they might bring the child up in the Christian life; and a general, but brief, blessing. This service is clearly derived from the 1662 'Thanksgiving of women after childbirth', but with Psalm 121 instead of 127[88], and the addition of a prayer for the child. Unlike 1662 there is no mention of 'accustomed offerings' or Holy Communion.

---

[88] Ps 121 was the only Psalm offered in the shorter 1549 service.

The second order is a general liturgy for thanksgiving, for use after an important event, such as 'recovery from an illness, an accident, or any other peril, or after a joyful event'; and this is paralleled in Congo's book.

Tanzania	Congo
The person giving thanks explains why	The minister explains who is giving thanks and why
Psalm 34.1–8 or Psalm 121	Psalm 111 or 145, or another suitable Psalm, or a 12-line responsary based on verse from the Psalms
A short prayer, adaptable to the event.	Either a General Thanksgiving (ASB) or a shorter, but similar, prayer
Blessing of the individual (brief); with a sprinkling of holy water 'where this is done'	A prayer of thanks for the specific event, ten options printed[89], where none fits the minister may use his own words.
The individual makes an offering	Hymn during which offerings are made
Holy Communion should follow	Blessing of the individual (Aaronic)

In Congo, this liturgy could stand alone but would often be incorporated into another service, and the thank-offering would be separate from the general giving of the congregation. The friends and family of the person giving thanks would normally also contribute; and some cynically suggest that church leaders encourage the use of this liturgy in order to boost church income.

These thanksgiving liturgies have their roots in 1662... but there seems to have been a common development in East Africa, in that the books of Tanzania, Congo, and Kenya[90] all have such liturgies. Congolese clergy tell me that there is a similar practice in Uganda, and are surprised that the Church of England does not have such liturgies. Clearly there is scope for further research here, looking for a common antecedent, and perhaps establishing a resonance with African traditional religion.

5.10 Ordination

Both books include ordination liturgies. Space does not permit detailed comparison, but simply a brief survey. T1995 provides three services, in the sequence: bishop, deacons, presbyters. C1998 offers two: first a

---

[89] For a wedding, confirmation, baptism, healing, childbirth, many years of marriage, success, promotion, New Year, and reaching the midpoint of the year.

[90] K2002 p209-223

service for the ordination of deacons and/or presbyters, and then one for a bishop. We shall see that Tanzania includes a few more 'high church' options in the ordination of presbyters, and makes a clearer distinction between presbyters and deacons, both in prayer and symbol.

Bishops. In Tanzania the bishop-elect has to make a series of promises from the Provincial Constitution, and then a series of promises from the diocesan constitution[91]; and he signs documents detailing these promises. The bishop-elect then answers eight questions about his calling, life and work. By contrast, in Congo, the bishop elect is asked seven questions about his calling, life and work, and then puts his signature to them - there is no mention of constitutions, but one of the questions ascertains obedience to the Canons of the Church. In both books, after the imposition of hands a Bible is given, and a staff, ring and mitre may be given. A further option in Congo is a cross. The Congo book provides some liturgy for the installation of the new Bishop, to used immediately if he is ordained in his own cathedral, otherwise 'he is to go there and be installed without delay, before continuing with his work.'

Congo's joint service. Although some have questioned the propriety of ordaining both deacons and presbyters in the same service, for fear of blurring the distinction between the two orders[92], the geography of Congo dioceses made it more practical to hold combined services.[93] The key features come in the following order: the duties of deacons, the duties of presbyters, questions to the diaconal candidates, questions to the presbyteral candidates, a litany, a song calling the Holy Spirit, the ordination of deacons, the ordination of priests.

Presbyters. T1995's service is comparable in substance to that above, but omitting the litany. In Tanzania, the new presbyters are given a Bible, but in Congo a New Testament.[94] Both books permit the addition or adjustment of clothing. T1995 permits the giving of chalice and paten, and the anointing of hands (which is described in detail).

---

[91]   Including one to retire between the ages of 65 and 70.
[92]   The 6th International Anglican Liturgical Consultation in 2001 commended 'ordination to one order alone at any particular service'. Paul Gibson (ed), *Anglican Ordination Rites, the Berkeley Statement: to Equip the Saints* (Grove Worship Series 168, Grove Books, Cambridge, 2002) para 2A6
[93]   It would be easy to derive separate services from the combined order if desired.
[94]   This was changed from a full Bible at the Bukavu workshop.

Deacons. In the Tanzanian service for deacons, there is no song calling on the Spirit; and although the words of ordination conclude with a Trinitarian formula, neither the substance of this prayer, nor a longer deacon-specific prayer earlier in the service, makes explicit reference to the Spirit[95]. In both countries, deacons are given a New Testament. In Congo, deacons may receive 'clothing to show their office', but no mention of vesture is made in the Tanzanian order.

5.11 Other material

What else do the two books have in common? A litany, the Athanasian Creed, and lectionary material. But even so, the provision of each differs.

T1995 directs that the Litany should be used 'at the time of Morning Prayer, or before Holy Communion, every Friday of the year, and at other times ordered by the Bishop'. An alternative text is given, for use when the litany is to be sung - and this version includes petitions addressed to Mary and the angels, and a petition for the faithful departed. Prayers, including the Lord's Prayer, that of Chrysostom, and the grace, are printed immediately afterwards, to complete the order. In C1998 the litany has six parts, of which the first and last are compulsory, but the others are optional. A rubric explains how it may be used as the core of short stand-alone service, concluded by the Lord's Prayer, the collect, and the grace, but these are not printed. No guidance is given regarding how often it should be used.

The two translations of the Athanasian Creed seem to be independent: that in T1995 has 42 numbered sections, while that in C1998 has 23 longer sections. T1995 details the days on which this Creed is to be used (as in 1662), while C1998 commends its occasional use during the year. In C1998 the words of condemnation towards the end are softened by a footnote, added at Bukavu, directing the reader to John 5.24-29 and 6.28-29.

The Sunday and festival lectionary in T1995 follows a two year cycle[96], that in C1998 follows a three year cycle.[97] Within the lectionary T1995 presents extra material for Ash Wednesday and Holy Week.

---

[95]   In C1998, before the imposition of hands for any of the orders, there is a brief prayer adapted from NZ1989, 'fill them with your Spirit, gentle as a dove, fierce as tongues of fire, that he may enable them in your work'.

[96]   As in the ASB, based on the work of the Joint Liturgical Group in the British Isles.

[97]   This was based on the Revised Common Lectionary, incorporating some of the modifications made by the Church of England, when it adopted RCL in the 1990s.

What does the Tanzanian book offer that Congo does not? Two items that would meet the needs of regular liturgical daily prayer:
- weekday lectionaries for Holy Communion (two year cycle) and Morning and Evening Prayer (each with a one year cycle).
- the last 191 pages of the Tanzanian book are dedicated to the Psalter, with psalms apportioned to morning and evening for each day of the month.

What does the Congo book offer that the Tanzanian does not? A number of features of pastoral value in a variety of situations:
- an order for use when visiting the sick
- a selection of prayers
- an order for the commissioning of catechists and evangelists
- orders for the opening of a new church, and the installation of a new incumbent
- notes on the vesture of ministers
- a catechism (*ad* NZ1989) and the 39 Articles of Religion (*cp* 1662).

Amongst the prayers are some specific to the context. A prayer for Africa, usually attributed to Bishop Trevor Huddleston[98]:

> God bless Africa,
> guard her children,
> guide her leaders,
> give her peace,
> for the sake of Jesus Christ. **Amen.**

Another remembers those 'who died to bring us freedom'. It brings to mind the soldiers, many of whom were young teenagers, who died in the 'liberation' war of 1996-1997, but has wider application:

> God our parent,
> we remember with thanks
> your children who died to bring freedom to our country;
> give us a courageous spirit,
> that we might follow their example of self-sacrifice,
> and so defend this freedom, in justice and mercy,
> that our children might grow up without fear;
> for the sake of your Son, Jesus Christ. **Amen.**

---

[98] An English member of the Community of the Resurrection who served for 13 years in South Africa (honoured by the African National Congress) and 8 years as Bishop of Masasi in Tanzania (honoured in 1994 by the Tanzanian government).

6. Comparison with Kenya

The Anglican Church in Kenya prepared a new order for the Eucharist, which was published in 1989, subsequently a booklet of 'Modern Services' in 1991,[99] and finally in 2002 a complete prayer book with a similar range of services to the subjects of this study.

Briefly, how do the books of Tanzania and Congo compare with that of Kenya? The obvious difference is that, although Swahili is the common language of Kenya, the Kenyan services were drafted and edited in English, but with an eye to future translation into Swahili. But having said that, let us compare the process and the contents.

All three books were attempts to meet the practical and spiritual needs of the national church not with a translation of services from elsewhere, but by local composition and adaptation. Each of the three books stands in a succession of local prayer books (in Kenya the previous batch of modern services were authorized in 1975); and bolder steps are taken in each generation.

If we try to compare the length of time involved in preparation, we should perhaps take the starting point to be the dream of a new book, and end point to be the finalizing of the text (even if publication followed a year of more later). By this standard, Tanzania might be deemed fastest, working from 1988 to 1992; that is four or five years. Congo took five years, from late 1992 to late 1997. Kenya however, took fourteen years, if we count from 1987 to 2001. Joyce Karuri's notes at the back of the Kenyan book[100] make it plain that the project took longer than was first hoped; but I suspect that this delay gave more scope for circulation of texts, experimentation and reflection, and the end result is a more mature book with fewer rough edges.

If we were to calculate the number of church members involved in the

---

[99] Comprising Morning Prayer, Evening Prayer, Baptism, and drafts of 'Admission to Holy Communion' and 'Confirmation and commissioning for service and witness'.
[100] pp299-307

drafting and revision of each group, Kenya would score highest[101] and Congo lowest, reflecting not only the relative sizes of the Anglican Church in each country, but also the relative ease of communication.[102]

Comparing the content of the three books, it is clear that Kenya has taken on board more of local culture than Congo,[103] which in turn was more inculturated than Tanzania. Kings and Morgan have documented some of this in their Study, but I might note here:

- references to the 'ancestors' or 'faithful ancestors';
- in the Eucharist, the final blessing adapted from an ancient litany of the Turkana tribe;
- in the post-communion prayer the concept of 'sitting at the feet' of the Father;
- in baptism the retention of anointing because of its significance in traditional religion.

---

[101] For example, Gitari refers to 'two years of experimental cathedral and college use' in the Preface to the Communion booklet; and a draft of the Eucharist was even used in England, before the text was published in 1989. Later on in the process, in 2001, care was taken to canvas 'opinions from a wide cross section of people' (K2002 p301)

[102] In Congo we had no effective postal service, and transport from one diocese to another was best accomplished by air.

[103] 'Anointing with oil not only follows the practice of the early church but also is a component of traditional initiation ceremonies.' (Notes introducing the service, p44)

7. Comparison with the ideals of Kanamai

The 'Statement'[104] of the consultation at Kanamai was an open-ended document that contained not only recommendations but also issues for further discussion. It nevertheless gave clear pointers for the Anglican Churches of Africa to follow.[105]

In terms of process, it commended both thorough preparation by observing the context in which the liturgy would be used, and thorough consultation with the users of the liturgy. In terms of content, it commended cautious use of local symbols and imagery, making contact with the local cultures but neither offending other cultures nor losing the connection with the worldwide church.

If we are to evaluate the two churches which are the subject of this study, it is clear that the Anglican Church of Tanzania did better in terms of process, because more people were involved in the initial shaping and drafting of the services. However, in terms of content, the Anglican Church of Congo did better, in that the liturgies include points of contact with the culture, for example, in the culturally relevant aspects of the wedding and funeral services.[106]

The time may now be ripe for Tanzania to take another step forward. Roger Bowen reports,

'The present Chairman of the Tanzania Litugical Commission, Bishop Mdimi Mhogolo, has expressed a clear intention to Africanize the Tanzanian Prayer Book in the near future. The result may be even more interesting than the present Kenyan forms, since the Tanzanians will be working directly in Swahili, not a European language.'[107]

---

[104] JLS 28, pp37-48
[105] Kenya acknowledges the value of Kamamai, K2002 p301.
[106] We cannot be harsh on Tanzania, since the Kanamai Consultation came too late for the revision process there. Tanzania can still observe parts of Kanamai in the way that the book is used.
[107] Letter of Roger Bowen, October 2006.

8. Reflections on expatriate involvement

In Congo and Kenya expatriate mission partners were key in the preparation of new prayer books. In Kenya Graham Kings played a very significant role in the early stages. In Congo I was privileged to be entrusted by the bishops with each successive stage of drafting through to completion of the process. I had valuable access to the sources in English, I had learned Swahili more from textbook than from market, and I had the technical resources to prepare and reproduce drafts of the services.

It might be asked, if the aim is to have a truly indigenous liturgy, should the process not be driven and managed entirely by the local church? I have three responses:

Expatriates who have lived in a country for some years, sharing ministry and worship with local Christians, should have absorbed some of the values of the culture – and may even be more aware of them, having come in from outside.

While the aim is to have a local liturgy, it has to be remembered that each church is part of the worldwide body of Christ, and the presence of representatives of 'the rest of the world' is important to maintain that link.

Many African church leaders struggle to survive on the salaries that they receive, and have to engage in farming or crafts. Few have the time to devote to liturgical reform, or when they have it has a low priority amongst the pressing demands of ministry. Karuri acknowledges that until she was financed to work on K2002 full time, the completion of the project looked unlikely.[108]

When I raised the ambiguities of expatriate involvement with Karuri some years ago, she responded as follows:
'It has been alright for mission partners to participate in the liturgical formation as long as they do not ignore the local input. However, it has been very necessary for the African team of theologians to go through the review process carefully and thoroughly, removing and adding things here and there so then the final work is finally theirs and not the missioner's.'[109]

---

[108] K2002 p300
[109] E-mail, May 1999.

9. Conclusion

Each national church succeeded in preparing a comprehensive and usable prayer book to meet its own perceived needs. While Tanzania had paid attention to the issues arising from it s two theological traditions, it had no energy to engage with questions of inculturation. Congo, on the other hand being more homogeneous in its theology and practice, was able to consider the needs of its cultural situation.

Dirokpa Balufuga was Bishop of Bukavu at the time of the preparation of the Congo book, and is now Archbishop. In his unpublished doctoral thesis he accuses the Anglican Church in Congo of having been 'timid' about meeting the local culture throughout its century of life, and asserts that the book of 1998 does not go far enough.[110]

There is no doubt that within another ten years, a new round of liturgical revision will take place, as leaders of each church seek to relate a changing church to a changing world. It may be that Tanzania is now able to draw upon the experiences of Congo and Kenya to engage with its cultural context. The Anglican Church of Congo may yet review how it can minister to a country traumatized by decay and warfare, but (hopefully) once more developing.

I invite you to pray with me for them, and to look forward to seeing how both churches will move on under God.

---

[110] *Liturgie Anglicane et inculturation hier, aujourd'hui et demain: regard sur la élébration eucharistique en République Démocratique du Congo* (Université Laval, 2001). The latter part of his thesis contains both textual and other proposals for further revision.

Appendix 1: Select Bibliography

1) Background reading on Congo, Tanzania and their churches

John F. Clark, *The African stakes of the Congo war* (Macmillan, New York 2002) / (Fountain, Kampala, 2003)

Maia Green,.*Priests, Witches and Power : Popular Christianity after Mission in Southern Tanzania* (CUP, New York, 2003)

Adam Hochschild, *King Leopold's Ghost: A Story of Greed, Terror and Heroism* (Papermac, 2000)

Irving Kaplan (ed), *Tanzania, a country study* (The American University, Washington DC, 1978)

Anne Luck, *African Saint: The Story of Apolo Kivebulaya* (SCM, London, 1963)

Roland Oliver, *The Missionary Factor in East Africa* (Longmans, London, 1965)

Andrew Roberts (ed), *Tanzania before 1900* (East African Publishing House, Nairobi, 1968)

Ruth M.Slade, *English-Speaking Missions in the Congo Independent State 1878-1908* (University of Louvain, 1958)

H. Maynard Smith, *Frank, Bishop of Zanzibar* (SPCK, London, 1926)

John V. Taylor, *Primal Vision* (SCM, London, 1963)

Michela Wrong, *In the Footsteps of Mr. Kurtz: Living on the Brink of Disaster in Mobutu's Congo* (Harper, 2002)

2) Reading on liturgy and inculturation

Gitari, David (ed.), *Anglican Liturgical Inculturation in Africa: the Kanamai Statement 'African Culture and Anglican Liturgy'* (Alcuin/GROW Joint Liturgical Study no.28, Grove Books, Nottingham, 1994)

Charles Hefling & Cynthia Shattuck (eds), *The Oxford Guide to The Book of Common Prayer: A Worldwide Survey* (OUP, New York, 2006)

David R. Holeton (ed), *Liturgical Inculturation in the Anglican Communion including the York Statement 'Down to earth worship'* (Alcuin/GROW Joint Liturgical Study no.15, Grove Books, Nottingham, 1990)

G.Kings and G.Morgan (eds), *Offerings from Kenya to Anglicanism: Liturgical Texts and Contexts including 'A Kenyan Service of Holy Communion'* (Alcuin/GROW Joint Liturgical Study no.50, Grove Books, Cambridge, 2001)

Phillip Tovey, *Inculturation of Christian worship: exploring the eucharist* (Ashgate, Aldershot, 2004)

3) Prayer books (other than those listed on page 2)

Anglican Church of Australia, *A Prayer Book for Australia* (Broughton, Sydney, 1995)

Church of Nigeria, *Order for Holy Communion or the Eucharist* (CSS, Lagos, 1995)

Church of Uganda, *Come and Worship* (Centenary, Kampala, 1992)

Appendix 2: Eucharistic Prayers

(The translation of the Tanzanian rite is guided by the 1981 translation of the 1979 rite; the translation of Congo A relates to the Church of England Series 3 which lay behind it.)

TANZANIA	CONGO A	CONGO B	CONGO C
The Lord be with you And with your spirit Lift up your hearts We lift them to the Lord And let us give thanks to the Lord our God. It is right and fitting for us.	The Lord be with you And also with you. Lift up your hearts. We lift them to the Lord. Let us give thanks to the Lord our God. It is good and right so to do.	Lord be with you And also with you. Lift up your hearts. We lift them to the Lord. Let us give thanks to the Lord our God. It is good and right so to do.	Almighty Father, you are with us at all times and in all places; we lift our hearts and voices to glorify your name: We praise your holy name!
It is indeed fitting and right for us, also our duty and joy, at all times and in all places, that we thank you, Holy Lord, Almighty Father, Everlasting God, through Jesus Christ our Lord. *[Words from Everlasting are replaced with a longer text on Trinity Sunday.]*	Indeed, it is best for us, it is our duty and our joy, at all times and in all places, to thank you O Lord, Holy Father, almighty and eternal God, through Jesus Christ, your only Son our Lord.	Indeed, it is our joy to thank you, O heavenly Father, for you created all things: the stars, sun, moon, and this world; hills and valleys, forest and field, rivers and lakes, and all that dwell in them.	Holy and perfect God, source of righteousness and truth; you are light, there is no darkness in you, and you hate all sin. We praise your holy name!
We praise you for the whole universe which you made and sustain through him, for the order of your creation, and for your many gifts of grace.	For he is your living Word, through him you have created all things from the beginning, and formed us in your own image.	You created human beings, making them more intelligent and powerful than all the animals; and you chose one nation to know more of you.	Loving God, friend to us sinners: you seek to gather your lost children beneath your wings; time and again you call us back to you. We praise your holy name!
Above all it is fitting, for us who have fallen, to praise you for your love, that you even gave your Son Jesus Christ, to take our human nature, that he might overcome sin and death and set us free, to become heirs of your kingdom.	Through him you have saved us from the slavery of sin, giving him a human birth, to die upon the cross, and to rise again for us. Through him you have made us your own people, exalting him to your right hand on high; and through him you have sent us your Holy Spirit of life.	We give you thanks, because when people scorned your will, you called them to return to your ways, by filling the prophets with your Holy Spirit, to be witnesses to your righteousness and power.	You sent your Son, to be born of the Virgin Mary, to be human like. us, but without sin, and you filled him with your Holy Spirit. **Thanks be to Jesus Christ,** **he came to save us!**

		He humbled himself to be the servant of all: he healed, he taught, he drew near to those whom others rejected. For the sake of our salvation, he died on the cross, rose from the dead, and ascended into heaven. **Thanks be to Jesus Christ, he came to save us!**
[Words from to take are replaced with alternative texts for Advent, Christmas, Epiphany, Lent, Passiontide, Easter, Ascension, and Pentecost.] O Father, we praise you for your Holy Spirit, who assures us that in baptism you have sealed us to be your own, so that we may proclaim your wonderful works.	*[Seasonal inserts are printed for Advent, Christmas, Epiphany, Lent, Holy Week, Maundy Thursday, Easter Day, Ascension, Pentecost, Trinity Sunday, and saints days.]*	With the words that the prophet Isaiah heard in the temple, we join with the angels and archangels, and all the host of heaven, praising you forever, saying,
Therefore with angels and prophets, with apostles and martyrs, and with the whole company of heaven, we glorify and praise you forever, saying (or singing):	Therefore with angels and archangels, and with all the company of heaven, we exalt and praise your holy name. We praise you forever, saying:	
Holy, Holy, Holy, Lord God of hosts, heaven and earth are full of your glory; glory be to you, Lord most high. Blessed is he who comes in the name of the Lord Hosanna in the highest.	Holy, Holy, Holy, Lord God of power and might, heaven and earth are full of your glory, Glory be to you, O Lord in heaven. Blessed is he who comes in the Name of the Lord. Hosanna on high in heaven.	Holy, Holy, Holy, Lord God of power and might, heaven and earth are full of your glory, Glory be to you, O Lord in heaven. Blessed is he who comes in the Name of the Lord. Hosanna on high in heaven.
Glory be to you, O heavenly Father, who in your great mercy gave your only Son Jesus Christ, that all who believe in him might have eternal life. Hear us, O merciful Father, we beseech you, that we, as we receive this bread and this cup, as your Son commanded us, may be partakers of his Body and Blood.	Accept our praises O heavenly Father, through your Son, our Saviour Jesus Christ, and as we receive this bread and this cup as your Son commanded us, may we be partakers of his body and blood.	We give you thanks, O loving Father, for you sent your Son, to be born as man, to show us your likeness, and to save people of all nations, by dying for our sake on the cross.

Appendix 2: Eucharistic Prayers

TANZANIA	CONGO A	CONGO B	CONGO C
In the same night in which he was betrayed, he took bread and, having thanked you and glorified you, broke it and gave it to his disciples saying: 'Take, eat, this is my body which is given for you. Do this in remembrance of me.'	On the same night that he was betrayed he took bread and, after giving you thanks, he broke it and gave it to his disciples saying: 'Take, eat, this is my Body which is given for you; do this in remembrance of me.'	On the same night that he was betrayed he took bread and, after giving you thanks, he broke it and gave it to his disciples saying: 'Take eat, this is my body which is given for you. Do this in remembrance of me.	Before his death, at table with his disciples: he took bread, gave you thanks, broke it, and gave it to them, saying: 'Take, eat, this is my Body which is given for you.'
Likewise after eating he took the cup, and gave thanks, and gave it to them saying: 'Drink of this, all of you. For this is my blood of the New Covenant, which is shed for you and for many for the forgiveness of sins; do this every time you drink it, in remembrance of me.'	In the same way, when they had eaten, he took the cup; and after giving you thanks, he gave it to them saying, 'Drink this all of you, for this is my Blood of the New Covenant, which is shed for you and for many, for the forgiveness of sins; do this, as often as you drink it, in remembrance of me.'	In the same way, when they had eaten, he took the cup; and after giving you thanks, he gave it to them saying, 'Drink this all of you, for this is my Blood of the New Covenant, which is shed for you and for many, for the forgiveness of sins; do this, as often as you drink it, in remembrance of me.'	Afterwards he took the cup, gave you thanks, and gave it to them, saying: 'This is my blood of the new Covenant, which is shed for you and for many, for the forgiveness of sins.Do this in remembrance of me.'
O Father, his death we proclaim his resurrection we affirm, his return we await. Glory be to you, Lord.	Christ has died; Christ is risen; Christ will come again.	Christ has died; Christ is risen; Christ will come again.	Thanks be to Jesus Christ, he came to save us!
Therefore, O Father, with this bread and this cup, we do this for the remembrance commanded by your Son Jesus Christ.	Indeed, heavenly Father, with this bread and this cup we do this in remembrance of him.	We give you thanks, because you fulfilled Jesus' promise, by sending us the Helper, the Holy Spirit, so that the Good News of your love might be known throughout the world.	He did not leave his friends like orphans, for your Holy Spirit came to comfort them, to sanctify them, and to empower them.

We proclaim his death as a perfect sacrifice, which he made for us on the cross once for all, and we celebrate the redemption he gave us. We thank you, O Father, for his mighty resurrection, and his ascension into heaven, where he is always interceding for us. And we look for his coming again in glory.	We show and proclaim his perfect sacrifice made once for all on the cross; we proclaim his resurrection from the dead, and his ascension into heaven; and we wait for his coming in glory.	And now, as we do this in remembrance of Jesus, grant, by the power of your Spirit, that we may be partakers of his body and blood.	Father, we thank you forever, because your Sprit gives us life, unity and strength. **May your Holy Spirit be with us every day!** Today as we remember Christ in this way, through the power of your Spirit may this bread be to us his body, and this wine be to us his blood, so that our hearts be made clean, and we may be ready to obey your will. **May your Holy Spirit be with us every day!**
And grant us in him, we pray, that we may be filled with your Holy Spirit, that we might be united in your Church, which you have gathered from all the ends of the earth;	Accept through him, our high priest, this our sacrifice of praise and thanks, and as we eat and drink these holy gifts, in the presence of your majesty, renew us by your Spirit, inspire us with your love, and unite us in the body of your Son.	Renew us through your Spirit, that we may, together with your church everywhere, serve our neighbours in your love, draw all people to you, and reveal your glory,	Revive your church, that it might be salt, yeast and light in the world, bearing witness to your holiness and love, while we wait for Christ's return in glory. **May your Holy Spirit be with us every day!**
through him and in him, in the unity of the Holy Spirit, all honour and glory be to you Father God Almighty.	With him and through him, by the power of the Holy Spirit, with all who stand before you in earth and heaven, we worship you, Father Almighty, now and forever.	Father Almighty, now and forever:	We will worship you, Holy God, without ceasing, on earth and in heaven, forever and ever.
Blessing and thanksgiving and power be to our God for ever and ever. Amen.	Blessing and honour, and glory and power, be yours for ever and ever. Amen.	Blessing and honour, and glory and power, be yours for ever and ever. Amen.	Alleluia, alleluia, alleluia! Amen.

Alcuin/GROW Joint Liturgical Studies

All cost £5.95 (US $12) in 2007 – nos. 13-14, 22-23, 29-30, 47-48 are double size (and price);
nos. 4, 9 and 16 are out of print

**The above are all published by Grove Books Ltd, Ridley Hall Road, Cambridge CB3 9HU
For nos. 59 onwards, published by SCM-Canterbury Press Ltd, see the outside back cover**